MAKING MONEY WHILE YOU SLEEP
(Starting A Company like Vistaprint.com)

Dr. Jacolby Bledsoe

ISBN-13: 978-1519395627
ISBN-10: 1519395620

This book is designed to assist you in starting your our company just like vistaprint.com. The book will give you step by step on how to get the website. How much to start up and so much more. It also has blue print on how to build your own screen press and more. Learn how to become your own boss.

Table of Contents

Starting your Business

This is not a hustle, gimmick, nor scheme. Your success is up to you! Learning how to invest in yourself is the key to changing your finances. Making money while you sleep is a real possibility; all it takes is time and a lot of effort. Many people will not tell you the secret to success. Also, most people think, when starting a business, it is very complicated. They believe it takes a lot of money, & that it takes money to make money. What if, I can tell you, not only the secret to building a company like vistaprint.com, custommink.com, or an online clothing store, but can tell how to do it with very little cost. I have had more than my fair share of businesses-some successes, and some complete failures; nevertheless, I never stopped learning. To this day, I have mastered learning how to successfully, run 30 plus businesses, and want to share some of this great information with you. I wish I could give you all that I have mastered in this one book, if so, though, this book would never end. I can show you how to build a custom T-shirt/printing without leaving home. I can teach you how to start this for less than $500. You can even start your our own tv network. Research is the number one component to having a successful business. Most people who become frustrated, and give up on their dream, did not do the proper research. Please allow me a few minutes to explain why researching the business that you want to do is so important.

Research

Even though this book may give you a ticket to success, research is still the most important thing that you can do. Proper research can make your business a success but, if you fail to do so, your business will be a complete failure. There are three kinds of research you have to do: 1.Product, 2.Clients, & 3. Location. I will deal with each one of these individually, so you can get a complete understanding of their importance.

Product

Do I have a great product? Do people need my product? How often would people use my product? Would my product bring me high overhead or low overhead? How much profit can I make off this product? First off can I say this " I love making money! I hate losing it!" My goal is to never break even. If I cannot make a hundred percent plus profit, or return on my investment on the item, I don't want it! You are in business to make money, point blank period! These questions are very important in order to have a successful business. I want to use a custom T-shirt/Graphic and

Design Company as the perfect example for research. Do I have a great product? Yes, my product would be custom T-shirt/Graphic & Design (something that businesses and people need for marketing, Family reunions, promotion, and more. Do people need my product? Yes, Temp services, schools, and more. How often would people use my product? If marketed right, I will have new clients every day. There are over 2,000 new business opening every week. There are millions of people who have ideas of starting a business, & I would like to give them the ability to fulfill those dreams. Question: Would my product bring me high or low overhead? It would be a low, because over 85% of everything will be done in-house, and wholesale. How much profit can I make off this product? I can do a t-shirt for $3.50 and charge $15 per shirt. This is business 101... Your product has I to make money--never ever should it lose you money. A great product opens a lot of doors to success but, that does not guaranteed it is a Cash Cow.

Clients

Will the clients buy my product or service? This is the important aspect to your business, & the key to whether or not you will make money.

Location

I have three words for you in this section: Location, Location, Location! The perfect location brings home the money! You better start singing this song when you are thinking about location Money, Money, Money, Money...Money! That's all I have to say on this subject. If you are in a community where there are a hundred companies just like yours, brother and sister, you need to move, or make your company stand out.

Next, I want to deal with Business plans. Let's call this: "Building a Game Plan." A business plan is a formal statement of business goals, reasons they are attainable, and plans for reaching them. A business plan may also contain background information about the organization, or team attempting to reach their goals.

Business plans may target changes in perception and branding by the customer, client, taxpayer, or larger community. When the existing business is to assume a major change, or when planning a new venture, a 3 to 5 year business plan is required. Also, within those 3-5 years, investors will look for the return on their investment during that timeframe. Here is the prefect business plan I have obtained from bbplan.com.

Next, let's talk about start-up costs. Depending on how you want to, you can start a T-shirt/Graphic & Design company like vistaprint.com 1 of 3 ways. Let me say this, the more you invest the more money you have intentions of making. You can start a business with just $20 a month, but if not investing it to have it make more money, then why are you in business?

Let us now, deal with low investing/Time saver:

This cost will run you $20-$2000 to start up.

First, let's get the hard part out of the way...Understanding how to Outsource: You need a domain name, hosting, photoshop, wordpress, and printing. I am going to cheat for a minute, so you can save time & money. Are you ready...it's called:godaddy.com. This site will give a (Domain Name, Hosting, and Wordpress). This will cost you about $15 a month or a $140 a year. Next, we'll get printing out of the way. I can give you a lot of ways how to get printing done... and not have a printer! I will give you wholesale printing sites, with no contact. For example, in order to do this with signs, you'll go to: (365signs.com). This is a wholesale company that sells all types of signs & car wraps. Another example would be for all your printing: bags, cup, pens, business cards, invitations, etc. For this, you'll go to: (zooprinting.com). They are free to sign up for. This company is an easy way to make money without any printing headaches.   Photoshop CC is $10 a month, just go to adobe.com. Now, you need to know how to use your wordpress, free web design software thatgodaddy.com supplies with your hosting. You will need to learn about plugin, and one of my favorite themes, the X theme. Here are the plugins you will need (Woocommerce, Business and Flyer, & Fancy Product Designer,) You can build your screen press printer... here is a blueprint that tells you how. This will save you almost $989. You can purchase a printer, if you'd like. The average cost is $979-$7000. This will give you 75% profit in T-shirt printing, (by having this machine), rather than outsourcing your T-shirts, where you will lose the 75% due to overhead. You can design everything to be outsourced, & your profit will be around 25% to 37%, because of high overhead.

Higher Profit

This cost will be between ($2,000- $20,000) profit (100%-135%)

Secondly, there is everything in- house. With this, you can rent a printer for $126 a month, plus a per print charge. I always shop around for everything

. Amazon and ebay are my best friends. So, let me give you a list of equipment that you will need in order to have a successful print business:

Vinyl Cutter

Heat Press 16x24

KONICA BIZHUB C360

Guillotine SG (Paper Cutter)

AUTOMATIC ELECTRIC

Srceen Press

Wholesale Company

www.statononline.com

www.uscutter.com

www.atlen.com

Business Plan for Graphic & Printing Company

Table of Contents

1.0 Executive Summary

The Metolius Agency is a Eugene, Ore. based graphic design and visual communications firm. Metolius will be concentrating on corporate identity of established companies. The targeted customer is a small- to medium-size company that has been established for five to 15 years. The company has done well with the business so far, but they are in need of a new corporate identity to allow them to move to the next level.

Metolius will operate out of a small office in the downtown area. For months one through seven, Kiev Lartiste will be the sole employee. By month seven, Kiev will be hiring an assistant to help with design work as well as administrative details.

Metolius will offer companies a fresh perspective regarding corporate identity and visual communication. Kiev has a unique background where he has business skills and creative skills. Most firms come solely from creative backgrounds. While this is useful for the crafting of logos and other devices of visual communication, it lacks the intuitive business mindset that Kiev brings to the firm. This competitive edge allows Kiev to bring both an aesthetic design focus as well as a practical, quantitative mindset that adds value to the service offerings by creating solutions that have both creative elements combined with rational, business ideas. This is useful since the clients are more business oriented.

Metolius will grow their customer base by providing clients with well-priced projects due to reasonably low overhead, creative, practical designs that add more value than competing graphical art firms, and superior customer attention. The Metolius Agency will reach profitability by month nine and generate $27,347 in profits by year three.

Chart: Highlights

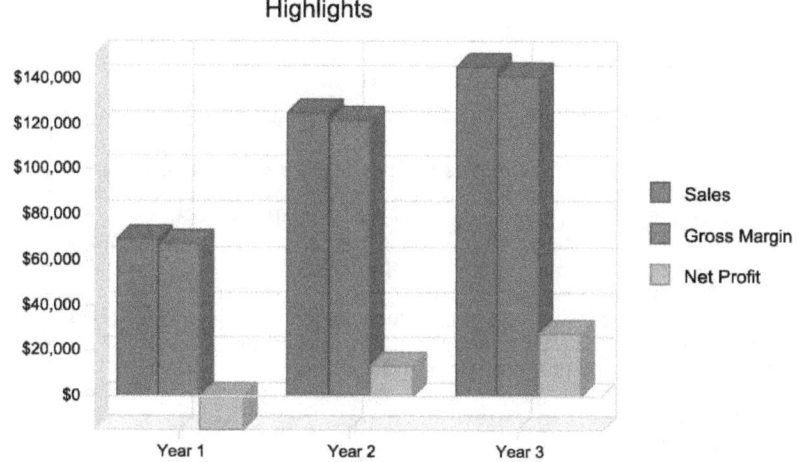

1.1 Objectives

The objectives for the first three years of operation include:

1. To develop a start-up graphics agency that will grow to profitability within year two.
2. To create a company whose primary goal is to exceed customer's expectations.
3. To create a firm that provides the target customers with valuable services and provides the owner with a flexible, creative, fun, and profitable business opportunity.

1.2 Mission

The Metolius Agency's mission is to provide the customer with creative and practical graphic design work and visual communication services. We exist to attract and maintain customers. When we adhere to this maxim, everything else will fall into place. Our services will exceed the expectations of our customers.

1.3 Keys to Success

The keys to success are:

- Professionalism
- Creativity
- Practical insight
- Enjoyment of the experience

2.0 Company Summary

The Metolius Agency is a start-up graphics firm that serves small- to medium-sized companies. The firm will be based in Eugene, Ore. and will operate from a small, downtown office.

2.1 Company Ownership

The Metolius Agency is a sole proprietorship owned and operated by Kiev Lartiste.

2.2 Start-up Summary

The Metolius Agency will incur the following start-up costs:

- Assorted office furniture including two filing cabinets, two work desks, a couch and two chairs for the waiting area, a round table with chairs, and assorted fixtures for the office.
- Two computers, each with 21" monitors, graphic tablet, black and white laser printer, inkjet color printer, scanner, CD-RW, and the following software: Illustrator, Freehand, Quark, Photoshop, Font Management Utilities, Traffic Office Manager (a scheduling and billing software), and Microsoft Project.
- Development of the website which will include design time by Kiev and implementation from a University of Oregon computer science graduate student.
- A current library of requisite magazines and journals.
- A DSL connection.
- Assorted office supplies.
- Stationary and brochures.
- Legal fees regarding business formation, creation of standard client contracts, and other general advice.

Page 2

Please note that the following items which are considered assets to be used for more than a year will be labeled long-term assets and will be depreciated using G.A.A.P. approved straight-line depreciation method.

Table: Start-up Funding

Start-up Funding	
Start-up Expenses to Fund	$1,000
Start-up Assets to Fund	$42,000
Total Funding Required	$43,000
Assets	
Non-cash Assets from Start-up	$19,800
Cash Requirements from Start-up	$22,200
Additional Cash Raised	$0
Cash Balance on Starting Date	$22,200
Total Assets	$42,000
Liabilities and Capital	
Liabilities	
Current Borrowing	$0
Long-term Liabilities	$0
Accounts Payable (Outstanding Bills)	$0
Other Current Liabilities (interest-free)	$0
Total Liabilities	$0
Capital	
Planned Investment	
Kiev	$43,000
Investor 2	$0
Other	$0
Additional Investment Requirement	$0
Total Planned Investment	$43,000
Loss at Start-up (Start-up Expenses)	($1,000)
Total Capital	$42,000
Total Capital and Liabilities	$42,000
Total Funding	$43,000

Page 3

Chart: Start-up

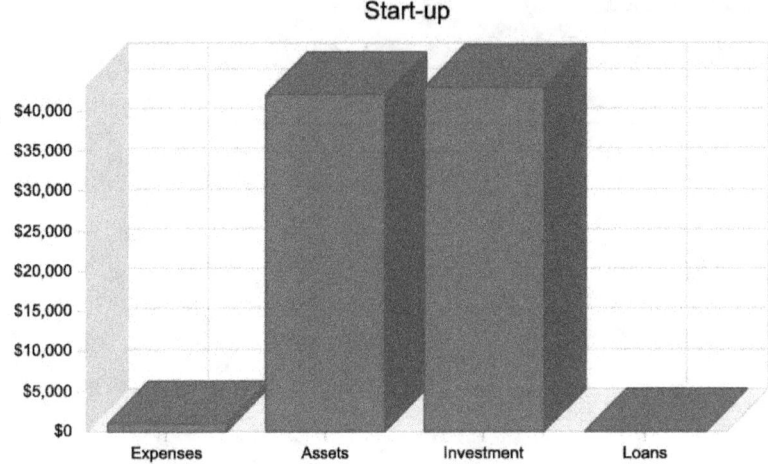

Table: Start-up

Start-up	
Requirements	
Start-up Expenses	
Legal	$500
Stationery etc.	$250
Brochures	$250
Other	$0
Total Start-up Expenses	$1,000
Start-up Assets	
Cash Required	$22,200
Other Current Assets	$0
Long-term Assets	$19,800
Total Assets	$42,000
Total Requirements	$43,000

Page 4

3.0 Services

The Metolius Agency provides graphic design and visual communication services to established, primarily Eugene-based, companies. Some of the services offered are corporate identity, marquees, logos, branding, and packaging.

The pricing of the projects are typically estimated as a project-based cost. The project cost will be estimated by the approximate number of hours needed to complete the project. Generally, Kiev will be charging $75 an hour for his services.

The majority of services will be provided at The Metolius Agency's office space. This office will be modern, practical, and sleek. This is very important because the office of a graphic designer is to a large degree a piece of their portfolio and reflects their work product. Therefore, a decent amount of money will be used to develop a proper appearing business office.

4.0 Market Analysis Summary

The Metolius Agency will be targeting small- to medium-sized companies. What these companies have in common is they have started as a small company with a good idea and have grown into a larger, more mature company that must now decide if they are going to maintain the current business strategy, or reinvigorate the company, employ professional service providers, and move to the next level.

4.1 Market Segmentation

The Metolius Agency has two distinct customer groups which they will concentrate on:

- Small-size companies: typically five to 15 employees
- Medium-size companies: 15 to 40 employees

These companies started with a valuable concept and leveraged their original grassroots visual communication elements. Now that they have matured into a larger company, they can no longer rely on the original grassroots corporate identity. These companies are in need of a professional firm like The Metolius Agency to expand their identify and take them to that same level as their competitors and be able to compete.

Chart: Market Analysis (Pie)

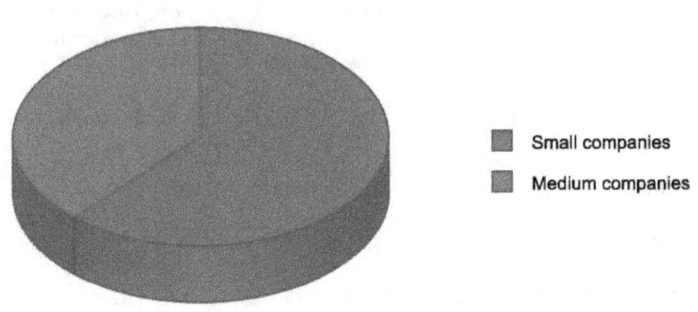

Market Analysis (Pie)

- Small companies
- Medium companies

Table: Market Analysis

Market Analysis							
		Year 1	Year 2	Year 3	Year 4	Year 5	
Potential Customers	Growth						CAGR
Small companies	8%	234	253	273	295	319	8.05%
Medium companies	7%	145	155	166	178	190	6.99%
Total	7.65%	379	408	439	473	509	7.65%

4.2 Target Market Segment Strategy

The market segments will be targeted in a number of different ways. It must be noted that graphics firms generate visibility and sales not through advertising, but through networking and client referrals. The methods used for the target market segment strategy will be:

- Networking. The networking will be based on leveraging Kiev's personal and professional relationships that he has developed after spending years in the industry. Ways of networking include sending out notecards to all acquaintances announcing the opening of The Metolius Agency, periodically meeting with people to catch up--as well to continue to network which means to find out who this person knows within the target companies that Metolius will try to turn into customers.

- Client referral. A lot of business is derived through referrals. Some of the referrals will come through the Chamber of Commerce, some of the referrals will come from customers. Recognizing that referrals will be a good source of new customers, Kiev will be in constant contact with the Chamber. In addition to being in contact with them, Kiev will investigate the possibility of doing a small project pro bono for the Chamber. This will be done to let the Chamber view an example of The Metolius Agency's work. It will also provide a reason for the Chamber to recommend The Metolius Agency. Kiev will work very hard to satisfy all

Page 6

of his customers. By making sure that he exceeds their expectations, he will increase the likelihood that he will receive referrals from satisfied customers.

- Targeted customer acquisition. This is the researching and strategic formulation to attract a chosen company to become a customer. Kiev will put together a list of 20-30 companies that would be excellent customers. Once these companies have been identified, Kiev will devise a strategy to target these companies as customers by initially determining what value Metolius can offer them. Eventually, the goal is to be able to meet with the decision maker of the company and present them with a portfolio of Kiev's past work as well as the proposed value Kiev can offer them.

4.3 Service Business Analysis

The graphic design industry is fairly diverse with all types of service providers. There are large advertising agencies, freelance designers, and in-house firms that typically only serve the specific company.

Within the last seven to 10 years, there has been a trend in the industry for the general advertising agencies, that previously only worked with advertising, to act as a full-service agency that not only prepares advertisements, but also does a lot of the creative work in-house instead of outsourcing it. This trend toward full-service agencies has continued. To a large degree it is occurring due to higher profit margins for the service providers. The Metolius Agency will be bucking this trend and concentrating on their specific skill set.

4.3.1 Competition and Buying Patterns

The following are examples of the different types of competitors:

- Large advertising agencies: over the years these firms have increased their number of service offerings from selling media forms of advertising, to a full-service company that develops creative work in-house, working with companies to develop corporate identity, etc.

- Freelance designers: these competitors are similar to Kiev because they are typically a one-man operation, often operating out of their own home. Often the freelance designers are just getting into the business and are trying to get experience, or they have left a firm in search of a more flexible lifestyle. Some freelance designers are well experienced and can offer the same professional level of quality the large agencies offer.

- Kinko's: while Kinko's is not a true competitor, it is a substitute competitor that should be mentioned. Kinko's stores do not have a true creative department, but for some of the larger accounts, it offers free creative services as a value-added feature to the larger customer. These services are typically provided by an employee who has introductory or intermediate skills using graphic design software such as Quark or Freehand, and in a small amount of time can generate creative images for the client. These services are typically not billed but used as a value-added benefit. While the price is quite good, the customer must recognize the fact that these services are not on par with a professional agency.

5.0 Strategy and Implementation Summary

The Metolius Agency's marketing and sales strategy will utilize networking and referrals to develop visibility for the company. Prospective customers will be turned into qualified sales through a professional showing that displays Kiev's portfolio of past work. The portfolio is key for making a positive impression regarding Kiev which illustrates his skill set and capacity as a creative designer.

5.1 Marketing Strategy

As noted previously in the target market segment strategy, The Metolius Agency will rely on three activities in their marketing efforts. These include:

- Networking: leveraging relationships to build more relationships within Eugene's relatively intimate community.

- Client referral: by providing outstanding customer attention, current customers are more likely to become a long-term customer and are more likely to refer their friends.

- Targeted customer acquisition: the first step of this process is to target who the ideal customer is, determine how Metolius can offer them value, and then network to come into contact with the decision maker at that company.

5.2 Sales Strategy

The sales strategy will be to utilize Kiev's portfolio of past work to qualify a sales lead. Using a portfolio is very common within the industry to show past examples of work. Kiev's strategy will be the development of several different portfolios, each one customized to a specific type of work. By having different portfolios, Kiev is able to better illustrate his proficiency with that specific skill set. In addition to the use of the portfolio, Kiev will do research on the prospective company and their industry so that he has specific knowledge of the needs the company may have and solutions that he can offer.

5.2.1 Sales Forecast

The first month of operation will be used to get the office set up and ready for business. Some of the time will be working with the interior designers to create a modern looking office space.

Months two through four will be somewhat slow as Kiev is developing clients. He is forecasted to take on some smaller projects. By month five Metolius will have developed larger projects and will continue to grow steadily.

Table: Sales Forecast

Sales Forecast	Year 1	Year 2	Year 3
Sales			
Small companies	$29,339	$50,697	$58,849
Medium companies	$40,058	$74,554	$86,543
Total Sales	$69,397	$125,251	$145,392
Direct Cost of Sales	Year 1	Year 2	Year 3
Small companies	$880	$1,521	$1,765
Medium companies	$1,202	$2,237	$2,596
Subtotal Direct Cost of Sales	$2,082	$3,758	$4,362

Chart: Sales Monthly

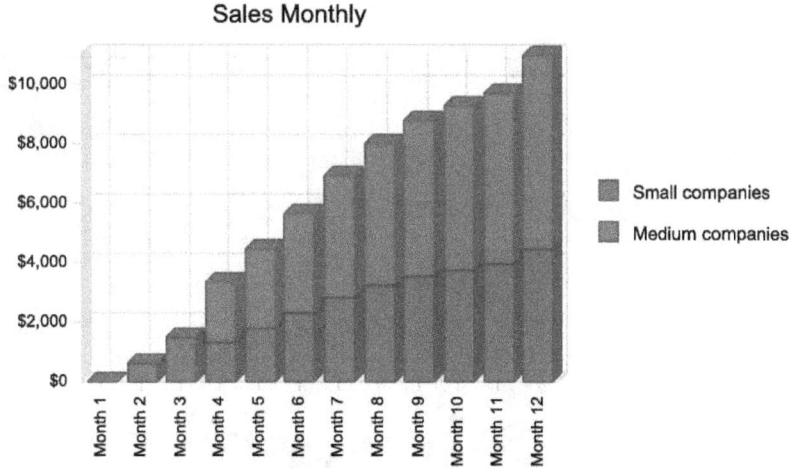

5.3 Milestones

The Metolius Agency will have several milestones early on:

1. Business plan completion
2. Office set up
3. Establishment of the first major account
4. Profitability

Table: Milestones

Milestones					
Milestone	Start Date	End Date	Budget	Manager	Department
Business plan completion	1/1/2001	2/1/2001	$0	ABC	Marketing
Office set up	1/1/2001	2/1/2001	$0	ABC	Department
Establishment of the first major account	1/1/2001	5/15/2001	$0	ABC	Department
Profitability	1/1/2001	9/31/01	$0	ABC	Department
Totals			$0		

Chart: Milestones

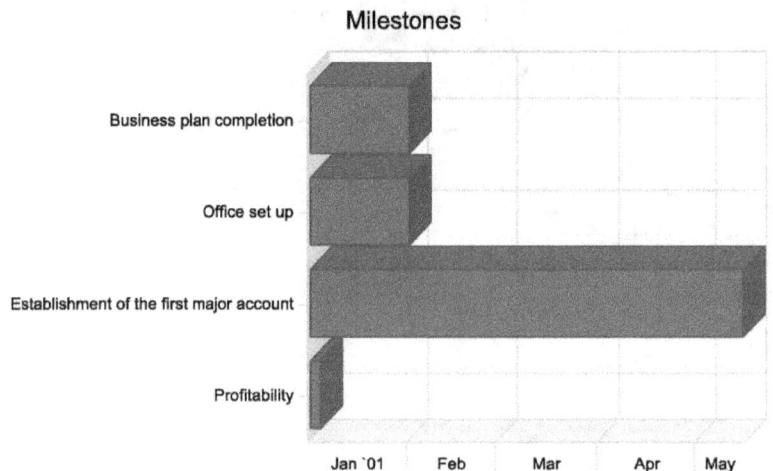

5.4 Competitive Edge

The Metolius Agency's competitive edge is based on Kiev's diverse background of business and creativity. Typically, most creative agencies are staffed by right-brain creative types. These people are extremely aesthetically oriented. While this is certainly an asset in the field of graphic design, it can be limiting because while their work might be extremely creative, it might not "hit home" with non-creative types which make up a large portion in the business world.

Kiev's background is based both in aesthetics and business. While Kiev always had a creative streak that he would use, his education was business oriented. This competitive edge allows The Metolius Agency to offer similar creative services other firms can offer, but also provide a unique business perspective.

6.0 Web Plan Summary

The website will be used as a way to disseminate information regarding the firm, show past examples of work, provide the interested party will several ways of contacting The Metolius Agency. In today's day and age, a website is almost a given, a standard source of information regarding the company.

6.1 Website Marketing Strategy

The marketing strategy for the website will be based on inclusion of the Internet address in all materials that The Metolius Agency releases, as well as submission to popular websites. Submission to search engines is an art in itself as different search engines work in different ways so a customized submission is most effective.

6.2 Development Requirements

A graduate student from the University of Oregon's computer science department will be used for the development (writing the code, Kiev will be responsible for the creative work) of the website as well as the periodic maintenance of the site. A graduate student will be used because of their expertise and typical below market rate.

7.0 Management Summary

Kiev Lartiste received his Bachelor of Arts in graphic design and business administration from the University of Oregon. While pursuing his undergraduate degree, Kiev was able to take several different graduate level business courses which were more challenging for him. While pursuing the double degree, Kiev began to recognize just how unique his skills were. Most of his colleagues in the art department had artistic skills equal to Kiev, but had no business sense. Likewise, his colleagues in the business department were very business oriented but struggled with creativity.

Upon graduation, Kiev went to work for Wieden & Kennedy in Portland. This was a wonderful experience as Kiev was surrounded by very bright, creative people. Kiev was given small projects, usually components of larger projects. While this was a good experience, he was unable to leverage his business skills under these circumstances.

After three years Kiev moved to Eugene and took a position with (name omitted), a large full-service advertising agency. The firm gave Kiev more management responsibility for his projects. After the third year, Kiev felt confident enough to entertain the idea of going out on his own and opening his own firm. After market research and writing a business plan, Kiev gave notice and opened up The Metolius Agency.

7.1 Personnel Plan

Kiev will be the sole employee through month seven at which time he will hire an assistant to help out with design execution, as well as some of the administrative details.

Table: Personnel

Personnel Plan	Year 1	Year 2	Year 3
Kiev	$42,000	$42,000	$42,000
Assistant	$17,280	$34,560	$34,560
Total People	2	2	2
Total Payroll	$59,280	$76,560	$76,560

8.0 Financial Plan

The following sections will outline important financial information.

8.1 Important Assumptions

The following table details important financial assumptions.

Table: General Assumptions

General Assumptions	Year 1	Year 2	Year 3
Plan Month	1	2	3
Current Interest Rate	10.00%	10.00%	10.00%
Long-term Interest Rate	10.00%	10.00%	10.00%
Tax Rate	30.00%	30.00%	30.00%
Other	0	0	0

8.2 Break-even Analysis

The Break-even Analysis indicates that approximately $7,000 will be needed in monthly revenue to reach the break-even point.

Table: Break-even Analysis

Break-even Analysis	
Monthly Revenue Break-even	$7,053
Assumptions:	
Average Percent Variable Cost	3%
Estimated Monthly Fixed Cost	$6,841

Chart: Break-even Analysis

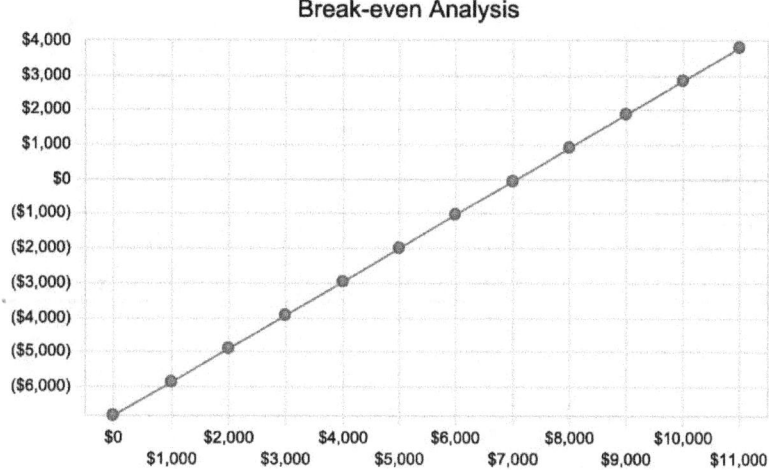

8.3 Projected Profit and Loss

The following table will indicate projected profit and loss.

Table: Profit and Loss

Pro Forma Profit and Loss			
	Year 1	Year 2	Year 3
Sales	$69,397	$125,251	$145,392
Direct Cost of Sales	$2,082	$3,758	$4,362
Other Production Expenses	$0	$0	$0
Total Cost of Sales	$2,082	$3,758	$4,362
Gross Margin	$67,316	$121,493	$141,030
Gross Margin %	97.00%	97.00%	97.00%
Expenses			
Payroll	$59,280	$76,560	$76,560
Sales and Marketing and Other Expenses	$2,820	$2,820	$2,820
Depreciation	$2,400	$2,400	$2,400
Website maintenance	$600	$600	$600
Insurance	$900	$900	$900
Rent	$7,200	$7,200	$7,200
Payroll Taxes	$8,892	$11,484	$11,484
Other	$0	$0	$0
Total Operating Expenses	$82,092	$101,964	$101,964
Profit Before Interest and Taxes	($14,776)	$19,529	$39,066
EBITDA	($12,376)	$21,929	$41,466
Interest Expense	$0	$0	$0
Taxes Incurred	$0	$5,859	$11,720
Net Profit	($14,776)	$13,670	$27,347
Net Profit/Sales	-21.29%	10.91%	18.81%

Chart: Profit Monthly

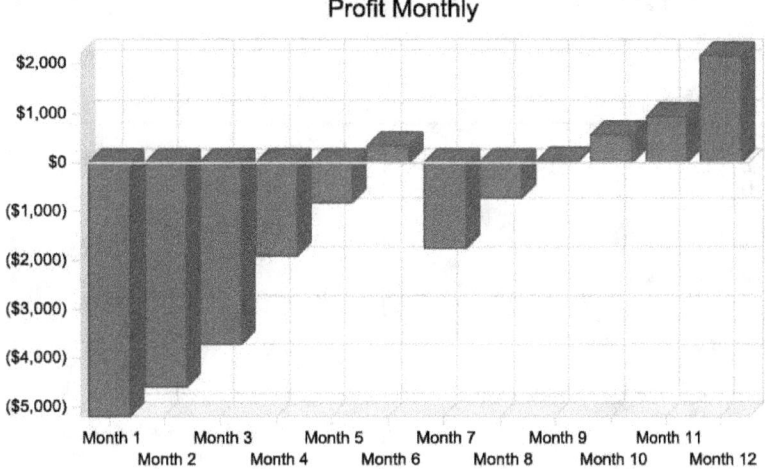

Page 15

8.4 Projected Cash Flow

The following chart and table will indicate projected cash flow.

Table: Cash Flow

Pro Forma Cash Flow	Year 1	Year 2	Year 3
Cash Received			
Cash from Operations			
Cash Sales	$69,397	$125,251	$145,392
Subtotal Cash from Operations	$69,397	$125,251	$145,392
Additional Cash Received			
Sales Tax, VAT, HST/GST Received	$0	$0	$0
New Current Borrowing	$0	$0	$0
New Other Liabilities (interest-free)	$0	$0	$0
New Long-term Liabilities	$0	$0	$0
Sales of Other Current Assets	$0	$0	$0
Sales of Long-term Assets	$0	$0	$0
New Investment Received	$0	$0	$0
Subtotal Cash Received	$69,397	$125,251	$145,392
Expenditures	Year 1	Year 2	Year 3
Expenditures from Operations			
Cash Spending	$59,280	$76,560	$76,560
Bill Payments	$20,322	$32,111	$38,554
Subtotal Spent on Operations	$79,602	$108,671	$115,114
Additional Cash Spent			
Sales Tax, VAT, HST/GST Paid Out	$0	$0	$0
Principal Repayment of Current Borrowing	$0	$0	$0
Other Liabilities Principal Repayment	$0	$0	$0
Long-term Liabilities Principal Repayment	$0	$0	$0
Purchase Other Current Assets	$0	$0	$0
Purchase Long-term Assets	$0	$0	$0
Dividends	$0	$0	$0
Subtotal Cash Spent	$79,602	$108,671	$115,114
Net Cash Flow	($10,205)	$16,580	$30,278
Cash Balance	$11,995	$28,575	$58,853

Page 16

Chart: Cash

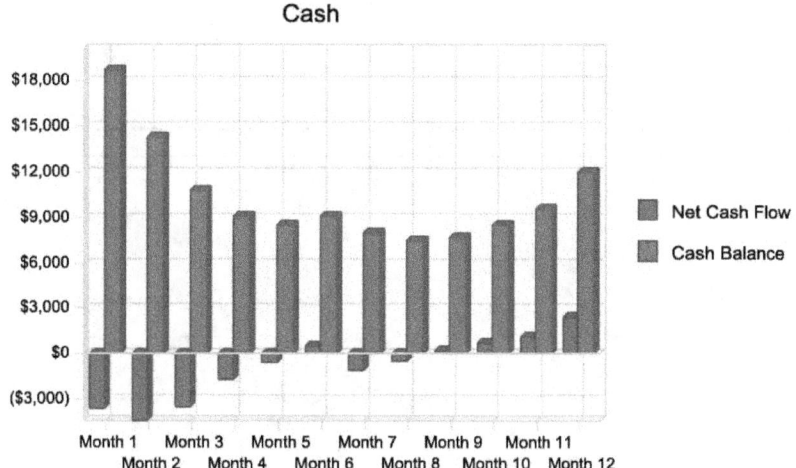

8.5 Projected Balance Sheet

The following table will indicate the projected balance sheet.

Table: Balance Sheet

Pro Forma Balance Sheet	Year 1	Year 2	Year 3
Assets			
Current Assets			
Cash	$11,995	$28,575	$58,853
Other Current Assets	$0	$0	$0
Total Current Assets	$11,995	$28,575	$58,853
Long-term Assets			
Long-term Assets	$19,800	$19,800	$19,800
Accumulated Depreciation	$2,400	$4,800	$7,200
Total Long-term Assets	$17,400	$15,000	$12,600
Total Assets	$29,395	$43,575	$71,453
Liabilities and Capital	Year 1	Year 2	Year 3
Current Liabilities			
Accounts Payable	$2,172	$2,681	$3,213
Current Borrowing	$0	$0	$0
Other Current Liabilities	$0	$0	$0
Subtotal Current Liabilities	$2,172	$2,681	$3,213
Long-term Liabilities	$0	$0	$0
Total Liabilities	$2,172	$2,681	$3,213
Paid-in Capital	$43,000	$43,000	$43,000
Retained Earnings	($1,000)	($15,776)	($2,106)
Earnings	($14,776)	$13,670	$27,347
Total Capital	$27,224	$40,894	$68,240
Total Liabilities and Capital	$29,395	$43,575	$71,453
Net Worth	$27,224	$40,894	$68,240

Page 18

8.6 Business Ratios

The following table compares standard business ratios with the Standard Industry Code #7336, Graphic Design Services.

Table: Ratios

Ratio Analysis				
	Year 1	Year 2	Year 3	Industry Profile
Sales Growth	n.a.	80.48%	16.08%	9.02%
Percent of Total Assets				
Other Current Assets	0.00%	0.00%	0.00%	52.57%
Total Current Assets	40.81%	65.58%	82.37%	76.45%
Long-term Assets	59.19%	34.42%	17.63%	23.55%
Total Assets	100.00%	100.00%	100.00%	100.00%
Current Liabilities	7.39%	6.15%	4.50%	34.45%
Long-term Liabilities	0.00%	0.00%	0.00%	23.62%
Total Liabilities	7.39%	6.15%	4.50%	58.07%
Net Worth	92.61%	93.85%	95.50%	41.93%
Percent of Sales				
Sales	100.00%	100.00%	100.00%	100.00%
Gross Margin	97.00%	97.00%	97.00%	100.00%
Selling, General & Administrative Expenses	118.29%	86.09%	78.19%	77.05%
Advertising Expenses	1.47%	0.81%	0.70%	1.42%
Profit Before Interest and Taxes	-21.29%	15.59%	26.87%	0.83%
Main Ratios				
Current	5.52	10.66	18.32	1.51
Quick	5.52	10.66	18.32	1.13
Total Debt to Total Assets	7.39%	6.15%	4.50%	66.33%
Pre-tax Return on Net Worth	-54.28%	47.76%	57.25%	2.06%
Pre-tax Return on Assets	-50.27%	44.82%	54.67%	6.12%
Additional Ratios	Year 1	Year 2	Year 3	
Net Profit Margin	-21.29%	10.91%	18.81%	n.a
Return on Equity	-54.28%	33.43%	40.07%	n.a
Activity Ratios				
Accounts Payable Turnover	10.36	12.17	12.17	n.a
Payment Days	27	27	28	n.a
Total Asset Turnover	2.36	2.87	2.03	n.a
Debt Ratios				
Debt to Net Worth	0.08	0.07	0.05	n.a
Current Liab. to Liab.	1.00	1.00	1.00	n.a
Liquidity Ratios				
Net Working Capital	$9,824	$25,894	$55,640	n.a
Interest Coverage	0.00	0.00	0.00	n.a
Additional Ratios				
Assets to Sales	0.42	0.35	0.49	n.a
Current Debt/Total Assets	7%	6%	4%	n.a
Acid Test	5.52	10.66	18.32	n.a
Sales/Net Worth	2.55	3.06	2.13	n.a
Dividend Payout	0.00	0.00	0.00	n.a

Appendix

Table: Sales Forecast

Sales Forecast		Month 1	Month 2	Month 3	Month 4	Month 5	Month 6	Month 7	Month 8	Month 9	Month 10	Month 11	Month 12
Sales													
Small companies	0%	$0	$600	$1,500	$1,360	$1,620	$2,296	$2,811	$3,240	$3,558	$3,769	$3,936	$4,450
Medium companies	0%	$0	$0	$0	$2,000	$2,676	$3,376	$4,134	$4,765	$5,232	$5,543	$5,788	$6,544
Total Sales		$0	$600	$1,500	$3,360	$4,496	$5,672	$6,945	$8,005	$8,790	$9,312	$9,724	$10,994
Direct Cost of Sales		Month 1	Month 2	Month 3	Month 4	Month 5	Month 6	Month 7	Month 8	Month 9	Month 10	Month 11	Month 12
Small companies		$0	$18	$45	$41	$55	$69	$84	$97	$107	$113	$118	$133
Medium companies		$0	$0	$0	$60	$80	$101	$124	$143	$157	$166	$174	$196
Subtotal Direct Cost of Sales		$0	$18	$45	$101	$135	$170	$208	$240	$264	$279	$292	$330

Page 1

Table: Personnel

Personnel Plan		Month 1	Month 2	Month 3	Month 4	Month 5	Month 6	Month 7	Month 8	Month 9	Month 10	Month 11	Month 12
Kiev	0%	$3,500	$3,500	$3,500	$3,500	$3,500	$3,500	$3,500	$3,500	$3,500	$3,500	$3,500	$3,500
Assistant	0%	$0	$0	$0	$0	$0	$0	$2,880	$2,880	$2,880	$2,880	$2,880	$2,880
Total People		1	1	1	1	1	1	2	2	2	2	2	2
Total Payroll		$3,500	$3,500	$3,500	$3,500	$3,500	$3,500	$6,380	$6,380	$6,380	$6,380	$6,380	$6,380

Page 2

Appendix

Table: General Assumptions

General Assumptions												
	Month 1	Month 2	Month 3	Month 4	Month 5	Month 6	Month 7	Month 8	Month 9	Month 10	Month 11	Month 12
Plan Month	1	2	3	4	5	6	7	8	9	10	11	12
Current Interest Rate	10.00%	10.00%	10.00%	10.00%	10.00%	10.00%	10.00%	10.00%	10.00%	10.00%	10.00%	10.00%
Long-term Interest Rate	10.00%	10.00%	10.00%	10.00%	10.00%	10.00%	10.00%	10.00%	10.00%	10.00%	10.00%	10.00%
Tax Rate	30.00%	30.00%	30.00%	30.00%	30.00%	30.00%	30.00%	30.00%	30.00%	30.00%	30.00%	30.00%
Other	0	0	0	0	0	0	0	0	0	0	0	0

Page 3

Table: Profit and Loss

Pro Forma Profit and Loss		Month 1	Month 2	Month 3	Month 4	Month 5	Month 6	Month 7	Month 8	Month 9	Month 10	Month 11	Month 12
Sales		$0	$600	$1,500	$3,360	$4,496	$5,672	$6,945	$8,005	$8,790	$9,312	$9,724	$10,994
Direct Cost of Sales		$0	$18	$45	$101	$135	$170	$208	$240	$264	$279	$292	$330
Other Production Expenses		$0	$0	$0	$0	$0	$0	$0	$0	$0	$0	$0	$0
Total Cost of Sales		$0	$18	$45	$101	$135	$170	$208	$240	$264	$279	$292	$330
Gross Margin		$0	$582	$1,455	$3,259	$4,361	$5,502	$6,737	$7,765	$8,526	$9,033	$9,432	$10,664
Gross Margin %		0.00%	97.00%	97.00%	97.00%	97.00%	97.00%	97.00%	97.00%	97.00%	97.00%	97.00%	97.00%
Expenses													
Payroll		$3,500	$3,500	$3,500	$3,500	$3,500	$3,500	$6,380	$6,380	$6,380	$6,380	$6,380	$6,380
Sales and Marketing and Other Expenses		$235	$235	$235	$235	$235	$235	$235	$235	$235	$235	$235	$235
Depreciation		$200	$200	$200	$200	$200	$200	$200	$200	$200	$200	$200	$200
Website maintenance		$50	$50	$50	$50	$50	$50	$50	$50	$50	$50	$50	$50
Insurance		$75	$75	$75	$75	$75	$75	$75	$75	$75	$75	$75	$75
Rent		$600	$600	$600	$600	$600	$600	$600	$600	$600	$600	$600	$600
Payroll Taxes	15%	$525	$525	$525	$525	$525	$525	$957	$957	$957	$957	$957	$957
Other		$0	$0	$0	$0	$0	$0	$0	$0	$0	$0	$0	$0
Total Operating Expenses		$5,185	$5,185	$5,185	$5,185	$5,185	$5,185	$8,497	$8,497	$8,497	$8,497	$8,497	$8,497
Profit Before Interest and Taxes		($5,185)	($4,603)	($3,730)	($1,926)	($824)	$317	($1,760)	($732)	$29	$536	$935	$2,167
EBITDA		($4,985)	($4,403)	($3,530)	($1,726)	($624)	$517	($1,560)	($532)	$229	$736	$1,135	$2,367
Interest Expense		$0	$0	$0	$0	$0	$0	$0	$0	$0	$0	$0	$0
Taxes Incurred		$0	$0	$0	$0	$0	$0	$0	$0	$0	$0	$0	$0
Net Profit		($5,185)	($4,603)	($3,730)	($1,926)	($824)	$317	($1,760)	($732)	$29	$536	$935	$2,167
Net Profit/Sales		0.00%	-767.17%	-248.67%	-57.32%	-18.33%	5.58%	-25.34%	-9.14%	0.33%	5.75%	9.62%	19.71%

Page 4

Appendix

Table: Cash Flow

Pro Forma Cash Flow		Month 1	Month 2	Month 3	Month 4	Month 5	Month 6	Month 7	Month 8	Month 9	Month 10	Month 11	Month 12
Cash Received													
Cash from Operations													
Cash Sales		$0	$600	$1,500	$3,360	$4,496	$5,672	$6,945	$8,005	$8,790	$9,312	$9,724	$10,994
Subtotal Cash from Operations		$0	$600	$1,500	$3,360	$4,496	$5,672	$6,945	$8,005	$8,790	$9,312	$9,724	$10,994
Additional Cash Received													
Sales Tax, VAT, HST/GST Received	0.00%	$0	$0	$0	$0	$0	$0	$0	$0	$0	$0	$0	$0
New Current Borrowing		$0	$0	$0	$0	$0	$0	$0	$0	$0	$0	$0	$0
New Other Liabilities (interest-free)		$0	$0	$0	$0	$0	$0	$0	$0	$0	$0	$0	$0
New Long-term Liabilities		$0	$0	$0	$0	$0	$0	$0	$0	$0	$0	$0	$0
Sales of Other Current Assets		$0	$0	$0	$0	$0	$0	$0	$0	$0	$0	$0	$0
Sales of Long-term Assets		$0	$0	$0	$0	$0	$0	$0	$0	$0	$0	$0	$0
New Investment Received		$0	$0	$0	$0	$0	$0	$0	$0	$0	$0	$0	$0
Subtotal Cash Received		$0	$600	$1,500	$3,360	$4,496	$5,672	$6,945	$8,005	$8,790	$9,312	$9,724	$10,994
Expenditures		Month 1	Month 2	Month 3	Month 4	Month 5	Month 6	Month 7	Month 8	Month 9	Month 10	Month 11	Month 12
Expenditures from Operations													
Cash Spending		$3,500	$3,500	$3,500	$3,500	$3,500	$3,500	$6,380	$6,380	$6,380	$6,380	$6,380	$6,380
Bill Payments		$50	$1,486	$1,504	$1,532	$1,587	$1,621	$1,671	$2,126	$2,158	$2,181	$2,197	$2,210
Subtotal Spent on Operations		$3,550	$4,986	$5,004	$5,032	$5,087	$5,121	$8,051	$8,506	$8,538	$8,561	$8,577	$8,590
Additional Cash Spent													
Sales Tax, VAT, HST/GST Paid Out		$0	$0	$0	$0	$0	$0	$0	$0	$0	$0	$0	$0
Principal Repayment of Current Borrowing		$0	$0	$0	$0	$0	$0	$0	$0	$0	$0	$0	$0
Other Liabilities Principal Repayment		$0	$0	$0	$0	$0	$0	$0	$0	$0	$0	$0	$0
Long-term Liabilities Principal Repayment		$0	$0	$0	$0	$0	$0	$0	$0	$0	$0	$0	$0
Purchase Other Current Assets		$0	$0	$0	$0	$0	$0	$0	$0	$0	$0	$0	$0
Purchase Long-term Assets		$0	$0	$0	$0	$0	$0	$0	$0	$0	$0	$0	$0
Dividends		$0	$0	$0	$0	$0	$0	$0	$0	$0	$0	$0	$0
Subtotal Cash Spent		$3,550	$4,986	$5,004	$5,032	$5,087	$5,121	$8,051	$8,506	$8,538	$8,561	$8,577	$8,590
Net Cash Flow		($3,550)	($4,386)	($3,504)	($1,672)	($591)	$551	($1,106)	($501)	$252	$751	$1,147	$2,404
Cash Balance		$18,551	$14,265	$10,761	$9,089	$8,498	$9,049	$7,943	$7,442	$7,693	$8,444	$9,592	$11,995

Page 5

Business Plan for Custom T-shirt Printing Company

Table of Contents

Table of Contents

1.0 Executive Summary

Your T-Shirt! is an exciting new business that allows people to custom design a shirt (specifically the design on the front or back) any way that they would like. By intelligently leveraging cutting edge technology, Your T-Shirt! will harness the power of computer sublimation to allow custom shirt printing in production runs as small as one unit. The company was founded by David Inkler. The company is set up as a Washington L.L.C. Your T-Shirt! will have a storefront in Seattle as well as a comprehensive website that allows ordering to occur anywhere.

Imagine the ability to create a totally custom shirt. You choose the material and style of the shirt, and then the image or graphic you want on the front and/or back. This is the ultimate form of expression. There are no limits to what you can communicate. Some people might show their fanaticism for a particular sports team, others a musician. Or you might have a social message or cause on your shirt. Whatever you may decide, you can print any image on your shirt.

Products

Your T-Shirt! will offer customers a variety of options for creating their own custom shirts. The majority of orders will be for t-shirts, however other style shirts will be available. Your T-Shirt! has developed a strategic relationship with Hewlett-Packard (HP) printer division. We will use their printer sublimation technology that allows a computer image to be applied to a shirt in a high quality, high resolution, economically feasible manner. This technology creates an image durable enough to withstand thousands of washings. Its photo-like quality, due to significantly higher printer resolution than anything on the market, will show off any image. The technology is cost effective enough to offer customers the ability to order just one unit. Most other competitors' costs prohibit printing custom shirts in one-off production runs. Finally, the customer may choose from an extensive library of existing images, supply their own image, or have an artist create an image for them.

Competitive Edge

Your T-Shirt! has two sustainable competitive edges to assist them in market penetration. The first edge is a enormous catalog of graphic images. By establishing strategic partnerships with companies that have existing graphic image libraries, Your T-Shirt! is able to offer an unprecedented number of options. Their second edge is the high quality of sublimation offered. From previous work experience, David has established close business and personal ties with HP's printer division and will exclusively be using prototype technology that offers an unprecedented high resolution sublimation process for shirts.

Management

Your T-Shirt! will be led by David Inkler and is not his first t-shirt venture. While in college David produced and sold tie-dye shirts. This early business experience gave David valuable insight into the market, the products, and the customer's needs and desires. Since leaving college David worked in Hewlett-Packard's printer division, and it was this experience that provided useful business and professional contacts within the shirt sublimation technology industry that he is currently leveraging. After three years in marketing at HP, David went back to school to earn his MBA. David will use his educational skills, his technological business contacts, and his previous shirt industry experience to make Your T-Shirt! profitable. Sales forecasts indicate that Your T-Shirt! will achieve sterling sales for years two and three respectively. Net profit will correspondingly be untarnished.

Chart: Highlights

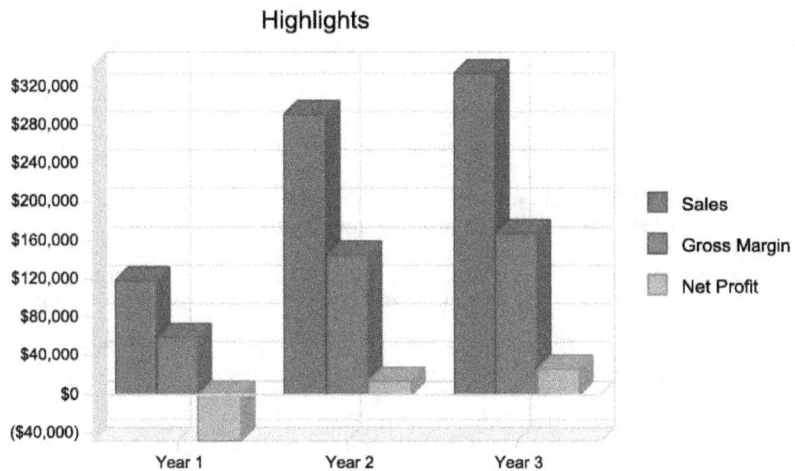

1.1 Objectives

- To become known as the premier custom shirt sublimation service.
- Achieve profitability within 12 months.
- Design and implement strict financial controls to help ensure success.

1.2 Mission

Your T-Shirt!'s mission is to offer the finest in custom shirt sublimation production. Your T-Shirt! will offer customers the best product at the best price. Customer's expectations will always be exceeded.

1.3 Keys to Success

- Leverage cutting edge technology as a competitive advantage.
- Exceed customer expectations by offering high quality products at reasonable prices with quick turnaround times.
- Employ careful financial and accounting analysis to ensure efficiency and proper controls.

Page 2

Your T-Shirt!

2.0 Company Summary

Your T-Shirt! is a start-up organization. It has been formed as a Washington registered L.L.C. by David Inkler. The L.L.C. formation was chosen as a way to minimize personal liability issues for the owner and avoiding the double taxation found in traditional corporations.

2.1 Company Ownership

David Inkler is the Founder and President of Your T-Shirt!

2.2 Start-up Summary

Your T-Shirt! will incur the following expenses for start up:

- Two Apple Macintosh computers -- These will be high end models and utilize the following software: Microsoft Office, Adobe Photoshop and Illustrator, Macromedia FreeHand, and QuickBooks Pro.
- HP XX Laser Printer -- This is a prototype printer not available to the public.
- In-store computer kiosk -- This allows customers to view options for shirts and existing imagery.
- Website -- This will be used for information disbursement as well as ordering.
- Shelving display unit -- To display assorted graphic images on paper for easier viewing.
- Broadband Internet connection.
- Two desk/chair/office supplies sets.
- Small shirt inventory -- Inventory will be kept small to lower overhead. This will be accomplished by using a shirt vendor who is one shipping day away, effectively using a just-in-time (JIT) system for managing inventory.
- Heat application unit -- To make the sublimation transfer.

Table: Start-up Funding

Start-up Funding	
Start-up Expenses to Fund	$17,100
Start-up Assets to Fund	$62,900
Total Funding Required	$80,000
Assets	
Non-cash Assets from Start-up	$6,500
Cash Requirements from Start-up	$56,400
Additional Cash Raised	$0
Cash Balance on Starting Date	$56,400
Total Assets	$62,900
Liabilities and Capital	
Liabilities	
Current Borrowing	$0
Long-term Liabilities	$65,000
Accounts Payable (Outstanding Bills)	$0
Other Current Liabilities (interest-free)	$0
Total Liabilities	$65,000
Capital	
Planned Investment	
D. Inkler	$15,000
Investor 2	$0
Other	$0
Additional Investment Requirement	$0
Total Planned Investment	$15,000
Loss at Start-up (Start-up Expenses)	($17,100)
Total Capital	($2,100)
Total Capital and Liabilities	$62,900
Total Funding	$80,000

Table: Start-up

Start-up	
Requirements	
Start-up Expenses	
Legal	$1,200
Stationery etc.	$200
Brochures	$0
Computer equipment	$6,200
Rent	$0
Insurance	$0
Office furniture	$1,000
Sublimation heat transfer unit	$2,000
Wesite development	$6,500
Total Start-up Expenses	$17,100
Start-up Assets	
Cash Required	$56,400
Start-up Inventory	$0
Other Current Assets	$1,500
Long-term Assets	$5,000
Total Assets	$62,900
Total Requirements	**$80,000**

Chart: Start-up

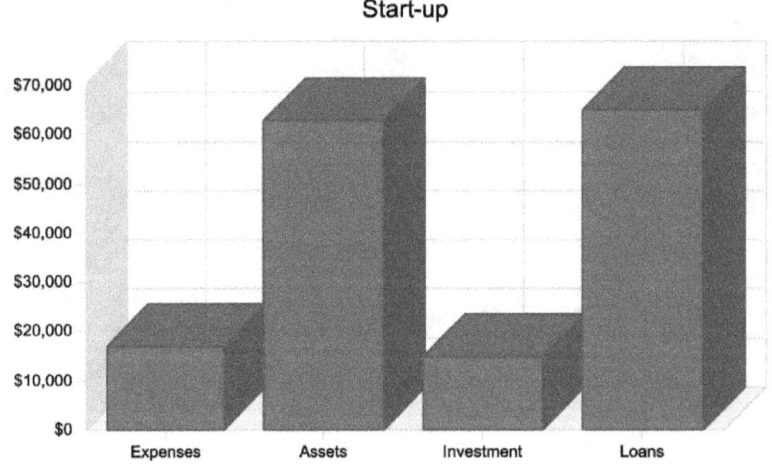

3.0 Products and Services

Your T-Shirt! is a custom T-shirt sublimation company that offering customers a choice of imagery (outs or theirs) to apply to the front or back of a shirt.

Sublimation is a process using heat to transfer (embed) ink into a fabric surface such as a shirt. The alternative method of creating custom shirt designs is called silk-screening, a process in which a screen is made with an image and that image is transferred onto a shirt. Because set-up costs are high silk-screening is not cost effective for small number production runs. Another disadvantage is that silk-screening applies a thin layer of ink to the surface the shirt inhibiting breathability. The sublimation process avoids this problem since the ink is not coating the fabric's surface, but rather, is embedded in the fabric. Only with recent technological advances has sublimation become cost effective in small production runs.

While other vendors are able to offer sublimation in single production runs, their computer based sublimation process produces lower image quality. Your T-Shirt! takes sublimation one step further by producing the graphic images at a higher resolution than other existing technologies. Through a strategic relationship with David's former employer, Hewlett-Packard, Your T-Shirt! has access to their new prototype sublimation high resolution printer giving Your T-Shirt! a significant advantage.

Your T-Shirt! will offer custom sublimation mainly on T-shirts, but will have other shirt styles available. Customers can choose from traditional cotton-blend shirts or all natural fiber cotton shirts.

Customers can then choose from pre-existing graphics or custom artwork. The pre-existing graphics are chosen from an extensive catalog. Your T-Shirt! has developed strategic relationships with several companies that offer a wide range of graphic images. The relationships allow Your T-Shirt! to list the other company's graphics within their catalog thereby significantly options. These images can be viewed and ordered online, providing customers with flexibility and convenience. Your T-Shirt! will have a comprehensive Website that will allow ordering a customer's home, or where ever they may be. Additionally, Your T-Shirt! will have a computer kiosk in the store front as an in-store catalog.

Your T-Shirt! will also offer custom artwork or graphic options for sublimation. The customer may bring in a graphic or may use Your T-Shirt!'s sub-contracted artist to realize their vision. Your T-Shirt!'s artist can take a customer's pencil drawing or even articulated thoughts and turn them into a new design.

Your T-Shirt! will offer a range of different shirt options. As indicated by the name, there will be an emphasis on T-shirts. Short sleeves, long sleeves, organic fabrics, and a variety of polo, rugby and other styles will also be offered.

4.0 Market Analysis Summary

Your T-Shirt! has segmented the market into two groups, organized by the type of product that they purchase. The first group is customers that desire an already created graphic image to be placed on the their shirt. The second group are those that prefer custom artwork to be placed on their shirt. Your T-Shirt! has decided to divide the market by the products that they purchase because it offers an intuitive, easy method of targeting the two different groups. An additional reason for segmenting the market based on the two products is because the demographics for the buyers of the two products are distinct enough to group them separately.

4.1 Market Segmentation

Your T-Shirt! has segmented their market into two distinct groups. As mentioned previously, the two segments are grouped by the type of product they chose. Although Your T-Shirt! is dividing the market by product type, it is effectively dividing the market by age as well since the customers who purchase the custom artwork shirts tend to be older than the group preferring the ready-made graphics. While this is not a hard and fast rule, it is a fairly accurate generalization.

Graphics -- This is group purchases a shirt and has an existing graphic placed on the shirt. This is the less expensive option and lends itself to low production numbers, as low as one, since there is not the inherent expense of artwork creation.

- Ages 14-25
- 69% are students
- Median individual income is $26,000
- Go out to eat 3.4 times a week
- Listen to 3.6 hours of music a week

Artwork -- This segment prefers having custom artwork created and placed on their shirt. They generally have the image or style in mind and will direct the artist to create it. Occcassionally when the customer will not have an exact image in mind but will rely on the artist's skills to help shape the work. Some of these customers will use Your T-Shirt!'s partner artist, others will have a friend or other service provider develop the art.

- Ages 24-43
- Median individual income is $42,000
- Go out to eat 2.7 times a week
- Listen to 3.3 hours of music a week
- 18% are using the shirt as a form of communication for a cause or a message

Table: Market Analysis

Market Analysis							
		Year 1	Year 2	Year 3	Year 4	Year 5	
Potential Customers	Growth						CAGR
Graphics	7%	7,879,664	8,431,240	9,021,427	9,652,927	10,328,632	7.00%
Artwork	8%	5,969,854	6,447,442	6,963,237	7,520,296	8,121,920	8.00%
Total	7.43%	13,849,518	14,878,682	15,984,664	17,173,223	18,450,552	7.43%

Chart: Market Analysis (Pie)

Market Analysis (Pie)

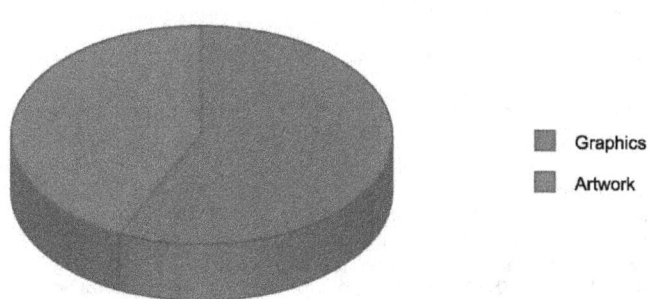

Graphics
Artwork

4.2 Target Market Segment Strategy

Your T-Shirt! has chosen these two market segments because their demographics (reasonably young) have the highest likelihood of purchasing a custom shirt. Both of these segments are reasonably young. This is important because most of Your T-Shirt!'s products are T-shirts and younger people tend to wear them frequently.

Music is also an important interest for the target markets since both segments listen to and watch more than average amount of music. T-shirts are particularly popular at music events. This phenomenon may be explained in part by the expressive nature of both music and T-shirt graphics. Your T-Shirt! will provide a form of expression, allowing each customer to choose what aesthetic or idea they want to communicate.

Lastly, the business will be located in Seattle which has a young, hip scene. There are many music and other venues that cater to Your T-Shirt!'s demographic and these will be useful in developing awareness of Your T-Shirt!

4.3 Service Business Analysis

The T-shirt design industry is a primarily brick and mortar based industry. Most companies offer either silk-screening or sublimation services to typically local customers. While most of the products are T-shirts, there is a niche of companies that offer these printing services for uniforms, team jerseys, etc. Most of the participants in the industry fall into two categories, those that sell to individuals and those that sell in multi-unit production runs. The companies that sell to individuals are almost always silk-screeners who have a limited number of silk-screens already developed. The customer chooses which one they want and a T-shirt is made. This type of vendor is often the typical T-shirt maker that you see at fairs. The second type of sells most of their products in larger production lots. This can be explained by the fact that for custom work, whether silk-screens or sublimations, it is not cost effective to produce in small lots.

Page 8

Recently, a number of companies began offering computer-based sublimation enabling them to offer low production runs. The technology the various companies are using, with Your T-Shirt! being an exception, are is in its infancy an is of low resolution. While the new technology allow companies to offer sublimation using computers, the image quality is average at best. Your T-Shirt! is able to leverage proprietary technology as a competitive edge to produce a much higher quality computer sublimation.

4.3.1 Competition and Buying Patterns

Your T-Shirt! has identified three competitors, two are local companies, the third is an Internet-based shirt designer.

- **T-shirt World** -- This local competitor specializes in silk-screening. 70% of their business is silk-screening with the remaining 30% sublimation. They require a minimum order of 10 with a 2-3 week lead time. This company only uses pre-existing designs for their silk-screening and for sublimations you must use their artist.
- **Shirt Shack** -- This local retailer is geared toward organizations or teams with production runs of 20 or more. They do fairly good work but are rigid regarding custom work.
- **Design House** -- This is an Internet-based retailer that primarily offers computer sublimations. Design House has a catalog of approximately 200 images for the customer to choose from. They do allow customers to use their own graphic. The quality of the sublimations is mediocre at best because they can only use off the shelf technology.

Another minor source of competition comes from home kits that turn your ink jet printer into a T-shirt making machine. While these kits do offer some competition, the image quality is not good, therefore this will only appeal to children or the home hobbyist, someone not very concerned with image quality.

5.0 Strategy and Implementation Summary

Your T-Shirt! will leverage their two competitive edges to quickly gain market share. The competitive edges are an unprecedented catalog of graphic images and the quality of their computer generated sublimations, a function of using prototype HP sublimation technology. The marketing campaign will emphasize the ability to completely customize a shirt. Youth events and student groups will be targeted. The sales campaign will emphasize making the experience as easy and pleasing as possible to encourage repeat customers and word of mouth referrals.

5.1 Competitive Edge

Your T-Shirt! has two competitive edges that they will use to their advantage to achieve market penetration.

- **Large catalog of graphics** -- Your T-Shirt! is developing several strategic relationships with existing graphics companies that have an extensive images catalogs. It would be difficult and expensive for Your T-Shirt! to create their own library of graphics but by developing relationships with companies who own existing libraries, Your T-Shirt! is able to offer its customers an expansive array of imagery. Your T-Shirt! pays a royalty for use of these graphics.
- **Quality of the sublimation** -- Due to its networking contacts at Hewlett-Packard, and the use of prototype technology, Your T-Shirt! will be able to produce sublimations of much higher quality than any of their competitors. This gives Your T-Shirt! a fantastic competitive edge. At some point within the next two years this technology may be available to the

public, however because of the close contacts Mr. Inkler shares with HP, Your T-Shirt! will always have cutting edge technology available, well in advance of any public release.

5.2 Sales Strategy

The sales strategy will emphasize the fact that ordering a shirt from Your T-Shirt! is a very easy and pleasing experience. The sales effort will work on the continual development of the website, the main tool used for ordering. It will be quite important to have a friendly, easy to use web interface for two main reasons. One, there are so many choices available that it could become daunting to the customer. The second reason is that a large portion of sales will be placed on the website. It is imperative to make it so easy that people don't stop part way through ordering due to cumbersome or difficult instructions. The website embraces the philosophy of making the experience so easy and pleasing that the customer comes back to buy more.

Your T-Shirt! will also rely on three other factors to help boost sales. The first is exemplary customer service. Having excellent service will provide the customer with the feeling that the business is looking out for the customer's interest. Second, when a customer places an order, they will probably be excited to see the finished product, so Your T-Shirt! will ensure the fastest turnaround time possible. Lastly, sales will be boosted by offering customers a high quality product. We will use high grade cotton shirts and state-of-the-art sublimation printing materials.

5.2.1 Sales Forecast

The sales forecast is reasonably conservative so that goals will be achievable. Sales will be slow initially, a function of the fact that Your T-Shirt! is a start up organization and it will take time to build a sufficient foundation. The following table and chart show sales forecasts by both month and year.

The sales forecast is broken down by product, graphics or artwork. "Graphics" indicates the customer will be using a pre-existing graphic, either one that they are bringing in or one that they are purchasing a license to use from Your T-Shirt! "Artwork" denotes that the customer is using a graphic that is being created specifically for them. All customers will purchase their shirt from Your T-Shirt!

Table: Sales Forecast

Sales Forecast	Year 1	Year 2	Year 3
Sales			
Graphics	$98,235	$242,151	$278,454
Artwork	$19,647	$48,430	$55,691
Total Sales	$117,882	$290,581	$334,145
Direct Cost of Sales	Year 1	Year 2	Year 3
Graphics	$49,118	$121,076	$139,227
Artwork	$9,824	$24,215	$27,845
Subtotal Direct Cost of Sales	$58,941	$145,291	$167,072

Page 10

Chart: Sales Monthly

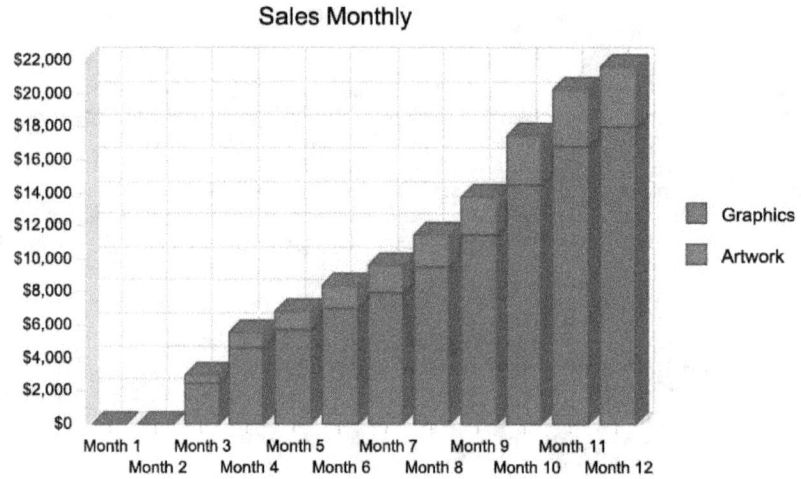

Chart: Sales by Year

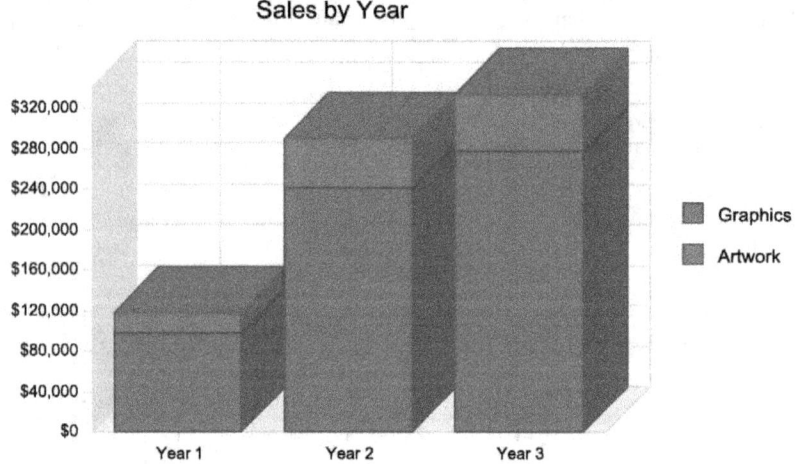

5.3 Marketing Strategy

The marketing campaign will seek to increase visibility for Your T-Shirt!, emphasizing the ability of the customer to completely customize their design. Your T-Shirt! will use several different venues to communicate this message.

Page 11

- **Advertising** -- Your T-Shirt! will run ads in several teen/young adult magazines whose readership demographics are similar to Your T-Shirt!'s.
- **Youth events** -- Many different events will be sponsored as a means of increasing visibility. These include but are not limited to music festivals and sporting events along with the new genre of extreme sporting events.
- **Student groups** -- Your T-Shirt! will attempt to gain awareness of the different student groups who actively purchase shirts for their members. Awareness will be achieved through a combination of sponsorship of student organization events as well as advertisements in magazines that specifically target this demographic.

5.4 Milestones

Your T-Shirt! has identified several milestones that are tangible and achievable. The milestones will serve as goals that the organization must reach to be successful. Please review the following section for details.

Table: Milestones

Milestones					
Milestone	Start Date	End Date	Budget	Manager	Department
Store build-out	1/1/2003	2/15/2003	$0	David	Construction
Website completion	1/1/2003	2/28/2003	$0	David	Web Development
First quantity order	4/1/2003	4/15/2003	$0	David	Sales
$50K in sales	9/1/2003	9/15/2003	$0	David	Sales
Profitability	12/1/2003	12/31/2003	$0	David	Accounting
Totals			$0		

Chart: Milestones

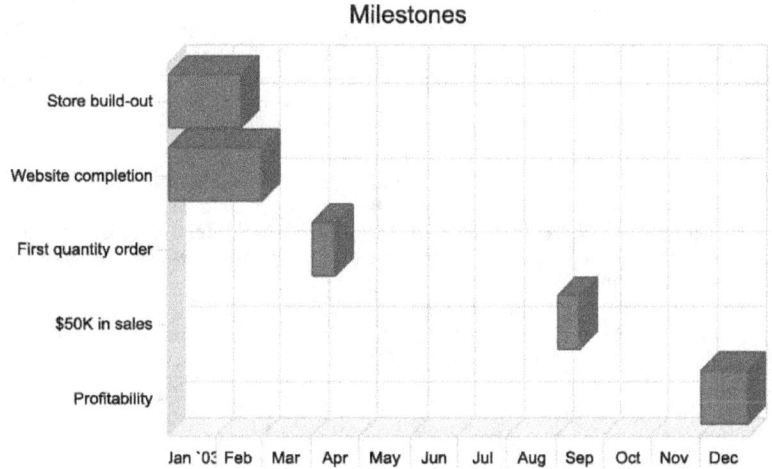

Page 12

6.0 Web Plan Summary

Your T-Shirt! will have a website developed that is based on the philosophy that the site must be user-friendly. Your T-Shirt!'s entire product catalog will be available on the site for customers to place orders. Because of the large volume of graphic image choices, it will be imperative that the site is easy to navigate through all the different options.

The store will have a computer kiosk for customers to access the graphics catalog. The customer can then place the order online or take the information to an employee to place the order.

The initial cost of the website will be the largest. Monthly maintenance costs will be marginal relative to the development and design costs.

6.1 Website Marketing Strategy

The website will be integral in Your T-Shirt!'s marketing effort as the site is a key sales tool for both local and distant customers. The URL address will always be used in promotional material, encouraging people to check out the company, concept, and the products. In additional to inclusion in the traditional marketing campaigns, Your T-Shirt! will submit their website to a variety of search engines, significantly increasing the number of inquiries from people searching out custom shirts.

6.2 Development Requirements

A computer programmer/designer has been identified as a candidate to manage the design, implementation, and maintenance of the website. The majority of the tasks will be completed by him, a few tasks that are outside of his skill set will be subcontracted to his associates.

7.0 Management Summary

Your T-Shirt! has been founded and will be led by David Inkler. David received his undergraduate degree in accounting/marketing from Seattle University. Upon graduation David moved down to Corvallis, Oregon and worked with Hewlett-Packard in their printer division. David spent three years with HP as a product marketing specialist, providing marketing assistance at a national level as well as being responsible for more grass roots, event specific marketing.

Recognizing that he did not want to spend the rest of his life working for someone else and recognizing that he did not have a sufficient skill set to start his own company yet, David enrolled in the University of Washington's MBA program. David did a cost benefit analysis and determined that it would be wise to take on debt and forgo two years of wages to be able to pursue his dream of opening his own business.

The completion of the MBA program forced David to then make some significant decisions regarding what business he wanted to start. While in college David had a few years of experience with t-shirts making and selling tie-dyed shirts to friends and at various music events. Within that niche, David quickly got a sense of what his customers wanted in tie-dyed t-shirts. Making the tie-dyes also gave David an outlet for his creativity.

When working for HP David became quite good friends with several of the unit leaders. It was these relationships that provided David with the opportunity to use cutting edge technology for

Page 13

his t-shirts. HP had been working on sublimation technology for several years, continually trying to increase the resolution quality. HP saw David's business idea as an excellent marketing project to test the technology and the business model. David and HP entered into an agreement where David would receive HP's latest equipment and in return David would provide HP with a wealth of product and marketing feedback. This appeared to be a win-win situation.

David's idea of developing a custom t-shirt printing business was a marriage of his business skills, his previous t-shirt experience, the leveraging of exclusive cutting-edge technology and his creativity. The more he thought about it the more he was convinced that this idea would satisfy his need for a challenging yet enjoyable job/business.

7.1 Personnel Plan

Your T-Shirt! will require the following personnel for operations:

- David -- Business development, finance and high level accounting, customer service, shirt printing
- Printer -- Shirt printing
- In-store retail employee -- Help customers with placing or existing orders
- Bookkeeper -- Accounts receivable and payable
- Independent contractor -- Graphic artist

Table: Personnel

Personnel Plan	Year 1	Year 2	Year 3
David	$22,000	$26,000	$30,000
In-store employee	$13,000	$13,000	$13,000
In-store employee	$7,200	$11,000	$11,000
Printer	$16,200	$21,000	$21,000
Bookkeeper	$10,000	$12,000	$12,000
Total People	5	5	5
Total Payroll	**$68,400**	**$83,000**	**$87,000**

8.0 Financial Plan

The following sections outline important financial information.

8.1 Important Assumptions

The following table details important financial assumptions.

Table: General Assumptions

General Assumptions	Year 1	Year 2	Year 3
Plan Month	1	2	3
Current Interest Rate	10.00%	10.00%	10.00%
Long-term Interest Rate	10.00%	10.00%	10.00%
Tax Rate	30.00%	30.00%	30.00%
Other	0	0	0

Page 14

8.2 Break-even Analysis

The Break-even Analysis indicates what will be needed in monthly revenue to reach the break-even point.

Table: Break-even Analysis

Break-even Analysis	
Monthly Revenue Break-even	$16,826
Assumptions:	
Average Percent Variable Cost	50%
Estimated Monthly Fixed Cost	$8,413

Chart: Break-even Analysis

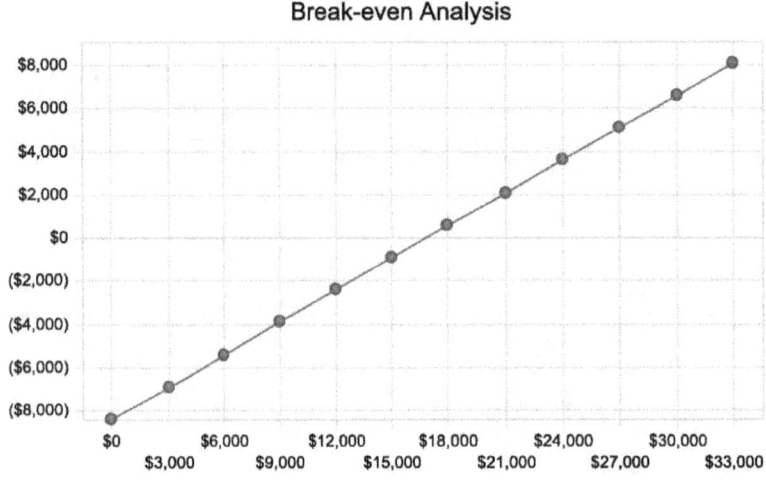

Page 15

8.3 Projected Profit and Loss

The following table presents projected profit and loss.

Chart: Profit Monthly

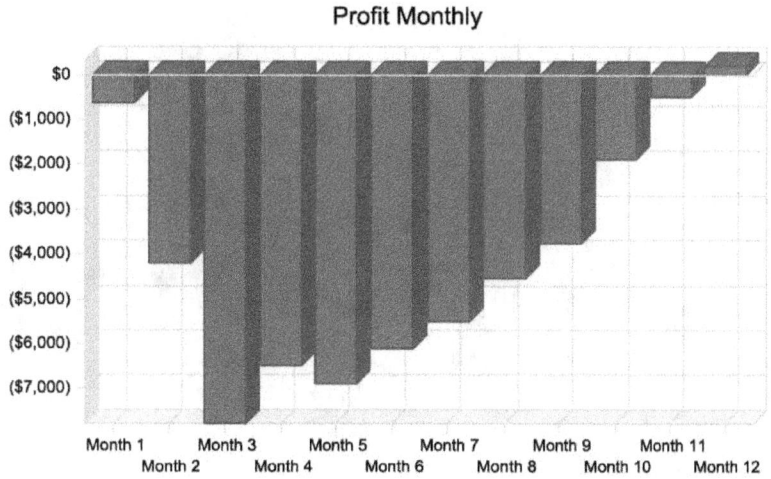

Chart: Profit Yearly

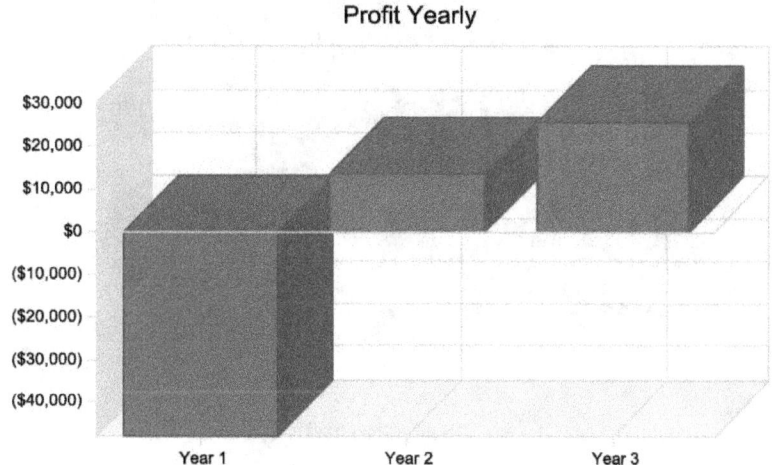

Chart: Gross Margin Monthly

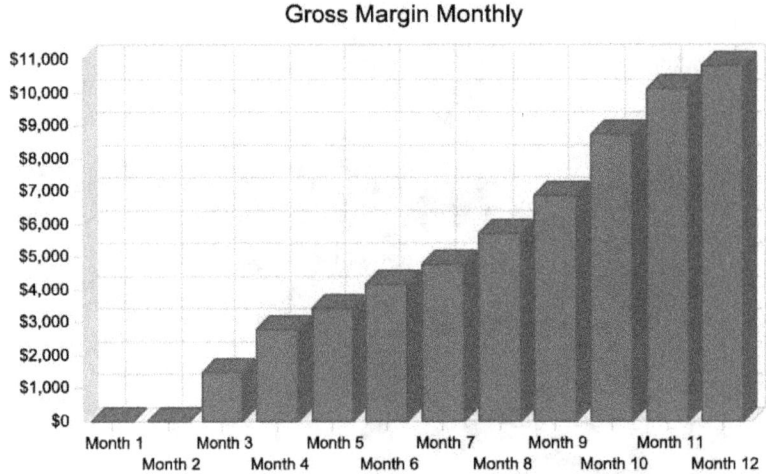

Chart: Gross Margin Yearly

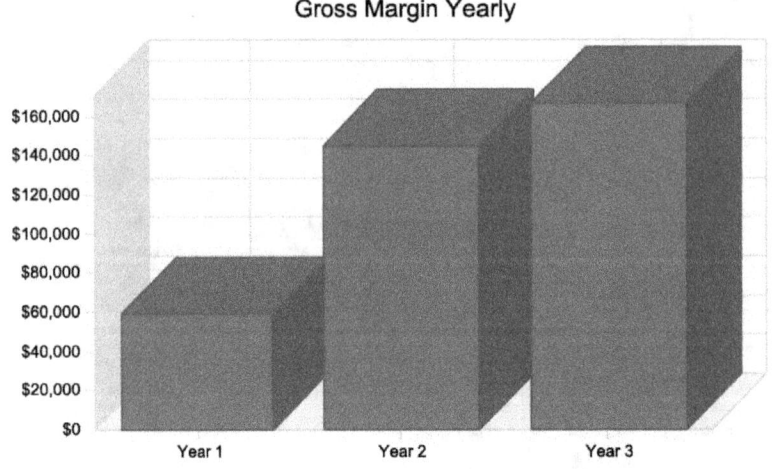

Table: Profit and Loss

Pro Forma Profit and Loss	Year 1	Year 2	Year 3
Sales	$117,882	$290,581	$334,145
Direct Cost of Sales	$58,941	$145,291	$167,072
Other Costs of Goods	$0	$0	$0
Total Cost of Sales	$58,941	$145,291	$167,072
Gross Margin	$58,941	$145,291	$167,072
Gross Margin %	50.00%	50.00%	50.00%
Expenses			
Payroll	$68,400	$83,000	$87,000
Sales and Marketing and Other Expenses	$2,500	$3,000	$3,000
Depreciation	$996	$996	$996
Rent	$11,000	$12,000	$12,000
Utilities	$3,300	$3,600	$3,600
Insurance	$3,000	$3,600	$3,600
Payroll Taxes	$10,260	$12,450	$13,050
Other	$1,500	$1,800	$1,800
Total Operating Expenses	$100,956	$120,446	$125,046
Profit Before Interest and Taxes	($42,015)	$24,845	$42,026
EBITDA	($41,019)	$25,841	$43,022
Interest Expense	$6,045	$5,700	$5,120
Taxes Incurred	$0	$5,743	$11,072
Net Profit	($48,060)	$13,401	$25,834
Net Profit/Sales	-40.77%	4.61%	7.73%

8.4 Projected Cash Flow

The following chart and table display projected cash flow.

Chart: Cash

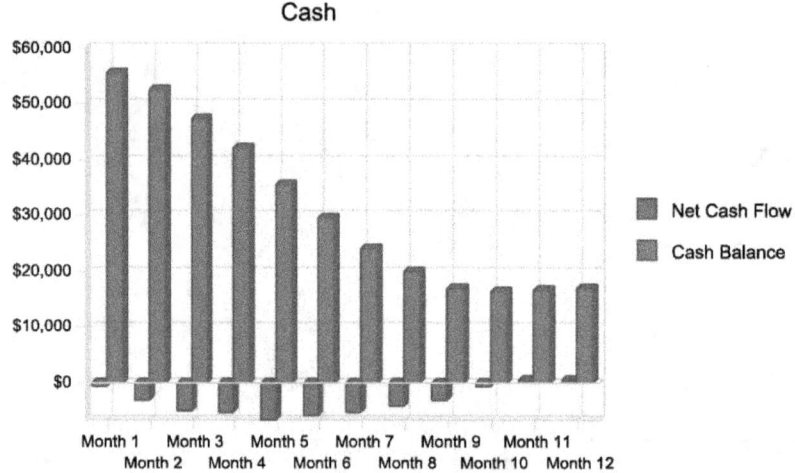

Page 19

Table: Cash Flow

Pro Forma Cash Flow	Year 1	Year 2	Year 3
Cash Received			
Cash from Operations			
Cash Sales	$117,882	$290,581	$334,145
Subtotal Cash from Operations	$117,882	$290,581	$334,145
Additional Cash Received			
Sales Tax, VAT, HST/GST Received	$0	$0	$0
New Current Borrowing	$0	$10,000	$0
New Other Liabilities (interest-free)	$0	$0	$0
New Long-term Liabilities	$0	$0	$0
Sales of Other Current Assets	$0	$0	$0
Sales of Long-term Assets	$0	$0	$0
New Investment Received	$0	$0	$0
Subtotal Cash Received	$117,882	$300,581	$334,145
Expenditures	Year 1	Year 2	Year 3
Expenditures from Operations			
Cash Spending	$68,400	$83,000	$87,000
Bill Payments	$80,550	$194,949	$214,783
Subtotal Spent on Operations	$148,950	$277,949	$301,783
Additional Cash Spent			
Sales Tax, VAT, HST/GST Paid Out	$0	$0	$0
Principal Repayment of Current Borrowing	$0	$200	$2,400
Other Liabilities Principal Repayment	$0	$0	$0
Long-term Liabilities Principal Repayment	$8,400	$9,000	$10,000
Purchase Other Current Assets	$0	$0	$0
Purchase Long-term Assets	$0	$0	$0
Dividends	$0	$0	$0
Subtotal Cash Spent	$157,350	$287,149	$314,183
Net Cash Flow	($39,468)	$13,433	$19,962
Cash Balance	$16,932	$30,364	$50,326

Page 20

8.5 Projected Balance Sheet

The following table shows the projected balance sheet.

Table: Balance Sheet

Pro Forma Balance Sheet	Year 1	Year 2	Year 3
Assets			
Current Assets			
Cash	$16,932	$30,364	$50,326
Inventory	$2,702	$7,461	$4,002
Other Current Assets	$1,500	$1,500	$1,500
Total Current Assets	$21,133	$39,326	$55,829
Long-term Assets			
Long-term Assets	$5,000	$5,000	$5,000
Accumulated Depreciation	$996	$1,992	$2,988
Total Long-term Assets	$4,004	$3,008	$2,012
Total Assets	$25,137	$42,334	$57,841
Liabilities and Capital	Year 1	Year 2	Year 3
Current Liabilities			
Accounts Payable	$18,697	$21,692	$23,765
Current Borrowing	$0	$9,800	$7,400
Other Current Liabilities	$0	$0	$0
Subtotal Current Liabilities	$18,697	$31,492	$31,165
Long-term Liabilities	$56,600	$47,600	$37,600
Total Liabilities	$75,297	$79,092	$68,765
Paid-in Capital	$15,000	$15,000	$15,000
Retained Earnings	($17,100)	($65,160)	($51,759)
Earnings	($48,060)	$13,401	$25,834
Total Capital	($50,160)	($36,759)	($10,924)
Total Liabilities and Capital	$25,137	$42,334	$57,841
Net Worth	($50,160)	($36,759)	($10,924)

8.6 Business Ratios

The following table displays many business ratios specific to Your T-Shirt! as well as industry ratios. Our SIC industry class is currently T-shirts, custom printed - 5699.0406. The following ratios are in variance to the industry ratios, please review the following explanations detailing the nature of the variance:

- Accounts receivable -- Your T-Shirt! does not extend credit
- Inventory -- Your T-Shirt! uses just-in-time (JIT) inventory management significantly lowering overhead
- Liabilities -- This business is being financed by debt, a long term bank loan
- Gross margin -- By leveraging the power of computer technology, labor costs are significantly decreased boosting the gross margin
- Sales/administrative expenses -- These expenses are higher due to the national reach of this organization and its target market

Page 21

Table: Ratios

Ratio Analysis				
	Year 1	Year 2	Year 3	Industry Profile
Sales Growth	n.a.	146.50%	14.99%	3.13%
Percent of Total Assets				
Inventory	10.75%	17.63%	6.92%	51.22%
Other Current Assets	5.97%	3.54%	2.59%	19.48%
Total Current Assets	84.07%	92.89%	96.52%	81.29%
Long-term Assets	15.93%	7.11%	3.48%	18.71%
Total Assets	100.00%	100.00%	100.00%	100.00%
Current Liabilities	74.38%	74.39%	53.88%	34.98%
Long-term Liabilities	225.16%	112.44%	65.01%	14.42%
Total Liabilities	299.54%	186.83%	118.89%	49.40%
Net Worth	-199.54%	-86.83%	-18.89%	50.60%
Percent of Sales				
Sales	100.00%	100.00%	100.00%	100.00%
Gross Margin	50.00%	50.00%	50.00%	38.96%
Selling, General & Administrative Expenses	90.68%	45.20%	42.02%	20.47%
Advertising Expenses	0.00%	0.00%	0.00%	2.95%
Profit Before Interest and Taxes	-35.64%	8.55%	12.58%	2.20%
Main Ratios				
Current	1.13	1.25	1.79	2.11
Quick	0.99	1.01	1.66	0.57
Total Debt to Total Assets	299.54%	186.83%	118.89%	4.52%
Pre-tax Return on Net Worth	95.81%	-52.08%	-337.84%	53.69%
Pre-tax Return on Assets	-191.19%	45.22%	63.81%	9.75%
Additional Ratios	Year 1	Year 2	Year 3	
Net Profit Margin	-40.77%	4.61%	7.73%	n.a
Return on Equity	0.00%	0.00%	0.00%	n.a
Activity Ratios				
Inventory Turnover	48.00	28.59	29.15	n.a
Accounts Payable Turnover	5.31	9.13	9.12	n.a
Payment Days	35	37	38	n.a
Total Asset Turnover	4.69	6.86	5.78	n.a
Debt Ratios				
Debt to Net Worth	0.00	0.00	0.00	n.a
Current Liab. to Liab.	0.25	0.40	0.45	n.a
Liquidity Ratios				
Net Working Capital	$2,436	$7,833	$24,664	n.a
Interest Coverage	-6.95	4.36	8.21	n.a
Additional Ratios				
Assets to Sales	0.21	0.15	0.17	n.a
Current Debt/Total Assets	74%	74%	54%	n.a
Acid Test	0.99	1.01	1.66	n.a
Sales/Net Worth	0.00	0.00	0.00	n.a
Dividend Payout	0.00	0.00	0.00	n.a

Page 22

Appendix

Table: Sales Forecast

Sales Forecast		Month 1	Month 2	Month 3	Month 4	Month 5	Month 6	Month 7	Month 8	Month 9	Month 10	Month 11	Month 12
Sales													
Graphics	0%	$0	$0	$2,500	$4,658	$5,689	$6,987	$7,989	$9,545	$11,454	$14,545	$16,858	$18,010
Artwork	0%	$0	$0	$500	$932	$1,138	$1,397	$1,598	$1,909	$2,291	$2,909	$3,372	$3,602
Total Sales		$0	$0	$3,000	$5,590	$6,827	$8,384	$9,587	$11,454	$13,745	$17,454	$20,230	$21,612
Direct Cost of Sales		Month 1	Month 2	Month 3	Month 4	Month 5	Month 6	Month 7	Month 8	Month 9	Month 10	Month 11	Month 12
Graphics		$0	$0	$1,250	$2,329	$2,845	$3,494	$3,995	$4,773	$5,727	$7,273	$8,429	$9,005
Artwork		$0	$0	$250	$466	$569	$699	$799	$955	$1,145	$1,455	$1,686	$1,801
Subtotal Direct Cost of Sales		$0	$0	$1,500	$2,795	$3,413	$4,192	$4,793	$5,727	$6,872	$8,727	$10,115	$10,806

Appendix

Table: Personnel

Personnel Plan		Month 1	Month 2	Month 3	Month 4	Month 5	Month 6	Month 7	Month 8	Month 9	Month 10	Month 11	Month 12
David	0%	$0	$2,000	$2,000	$2,000	$2,000	$2,000	$2,000	$2,000	$2,000	$2,000	$2,000	$2,000
In-store employee	0%	$0	$0	$1,300	$1,300	$1,300	$1,300	$1,300	$1,300	$1,300	$1,300	$1,300	$1,300
In-store employee	0%	$0	$0	$0	$0	$900	$900	$900	$900	$900	$900	$900	$900
Printer	0%	$0	$0	$1,500	$1,500	$1,500	$1,500	$1,500	$1,500	$1,800	$1,800	$1,800	$1,800
Bookkeeper	0%	$0	$0	$1,000	$1,000	$1,000	$1,000	$1,000	$1,000	$1,000	$1,000	$1,000	$1,000
Total People		0	1	4	4	5	5	5	5	5	5	5	5
Total Payroll		$0	$2,000	$5,800	$5,800	$6,700	$6,700	$6,700	$6,700	$7,000	$7,000	$7,000	$7,000

Appendix

Table: General Assumptions

General Assumptions		Month 1	Month 2	Month 3	Month 4	Month 5	Month 6	Month 7	Month 8	Month 9	Month 10	Month 11	Month 12
Plan Month		1	2	3	4	5	6	7	8	9	10	11	12
Current Interest Rate		10.00%	10.00%	10.00%	10.00%	10.00%	10.00%	10.00%	10.00%	10.00%	10.00%	10.00%	10.00%
Long-term Interest Rate		10.00%	10.00%	10.00%	10.00%	10.00%	10.00%	10.00%	10.00%	10.00%	10.00%	10.00%	10.00%
Tax Rate		30.00%	30.00%	30.00%	30.00%	30.00%	30.00%	30.00%	30.00%	30.00%	30.00%	30.00%	30.00%
Other		0	0	0	0	0	0	0	0	0	0	0	0

Page 3

Table: Profit and Loss

Pro Forma Profit and Loss		Month 1	Month 2	Month 3	Month 4	Month 5	Month 6	Month 7	Month 8	Month 9	Month 10	Month 11	Month 12
Sales		$0	$0	$3,000	$5,590	$6,827	$8,384	$9,587	$11,454	$13,745	$17,454	$20,230	$21,612
Direct Cost of Sales		$0	$0	$1,500	$2,795	$3,413	$4,192	$4,793	$5,727	$6,872	$8,727	$10,115	$10,806
Other Costs of Goods		$0	$0	$0	$0	$0	$0	$0	$0	$0	$0	$0	$0
Total Cost of Sales		$0	$0	$1,500	$2,795	$3,413	$4,192	$4,793	$5,727	$6,872	$8,727	$10,115	$10,806
Gross Margin		$0	$0	$1,500	$2,795	$3,413	$4,192	$4,793	$5,727	$6,872	$8,727	$10,115	$10,806
Gross Margin %		0.00%	0.00%	50.00%	50.00%	50.00%	50.00%	50.00%	50.00%	50.00%	50.00%	50.00%	50.00%
Expenses													
Payroll		$0	$2,000	$5,800	$5,800	$6,700	$6,700	$6,700	$6,700	$7,000	$7,000	$7,000	$7,000
Sales and Marketing and Other Expenses		$0	$0	$250	$250	$250	$250	$250	$250	$250	$250	$250	$250
Depreciation		$83	$83	$83	$83	$83	$83	$83	$83	$83	$83	$83	$83
Rent		$0	$1,000	$1,000	$1,000	$1,000	$1,000	$1,000	$1,000	$1,000	$1,000	$1,000	$1,000
Utilities		$0	$300	$300	$300	$300	$300	$300	$300	$300	$300	$300	$300
Insurance		$0	$0	$300	$300	$300	$300	$300	$300	$300	$300	$300	$300
Payroll Taxes	15%	$0	$300	$870	$870	$1,005	$1,005	$1,005	$1,005	$1,050	$1,050	$1,050	$1,050
Other		$0	$0	$150	$150	$150	$150	$150	$150	$150	$150	$150	$150
Total Operating Expenses		$83	$3,683	$8,753	$8,753	$9,788	$9,788	$9,788	$9,788	$10,133	$10,133	$10,133	$10,133
Profit Before Interest and Taxes		($83)	($3,683)	($7,253)	($5,958)	($6,375)	($5,596)	($4,995)	($4,061)	($3,261)	($1,406)	($18)	$673
EBITDA		$0	($3,600)	($7,170)	($5,875)	($6,292)	($5,513)	($4,912)	($3,978)	($3,178)	($1,323)	$65	$756
Interest Expense		$536	$530	$524	$518	$513	$507	$501	$495	$489	$483	$478	$472
Taxes Incurred		$0	$0	$0	$0	$0	$0	$0	$0	$0	$0	$0	$0
Net Profit		($619)	($4,213)	($7,777)	($6,477)	($6,887)	($6,102)	($5,495)	($4,556)	($3,750)	($1,889)	($496)	$201
Net Profit/Sales		0.00%	0.00%	-259.24%	-115.87%	-100.88%	-72.78%	-57.32%	-39.78%	-27.26%	-10.82%	-2.45%	0.93%

Appendix

Table: Cash Flow

Pro Forma Cash Flow		Month 1	Month 2	Month 3	Month 4	Month 5	Month 6	Month 7	Month 8	Month 9	Month 10	Month 11	Month 12
Cash Received													
Cash from Operations													
Cash Sales		$0	$0	$3,000	$5,590	$6,827	$8,384	$9,587	$11,454	$13,745	$17,454	$20,230	$21,612
Subtotal Cash from Operations		$0	$0	$3,000	$5,590	$6,827	$8,384	$9,587	$11,454	$13,745	$17,454	$20,230	$21,612
Additional Cash Received													
Sales Tax, VAT, HST/GST Received	0.00%	$0	$0	$0	$0	$0	$0	$0	$0	$0	$0	$0	$0
New Current Borrowing		$0	$0	$0	$0	$0	$0	$0	$0	$0	$0	$0	$0
New Other Liabilities (interest-free)		$0	$0	$0	$0	$0	$0	$0	$0	$0	$0	$0	$0
New Long-term Liabilities		$0	$0	$0	$0	$0	$0	$0	$0	$0	$0	$0	$0
Sales of Other Current Assets		$0	$0	$0	$0	$0	$0	$0	$0	$0	$0	$0	$0
Sales of Long-term Assets		$0	$0	$0	$0	$0	$0	$0	$0	$0	$0	$0	$0
New Investment Received		$0	$0	$0	$0	$0	$0	$0	$0	$0	$0	$0	$0
Subtotal Cash Received		$0	$0	$3,000	$5,590	$6,827	$8,384	$9,587	$11,454	$13,745	$17,454	$20,230	$21,612
Expenditures		Month 1	Month 2	Month 3	Month 4	Month 5	Month 6	Month 7	Month 8	Month 9	Month 10	Month 11	Month 12
Expenditures from Operations													
Cash Spending		$0	$2,000	$5,800	$5,800	$6,700	$6,700	$6,700	$6,700	$7,000	$7,000	$7,000	$7,000
Bill Payments		$0	$375	$1,652	$4,327	$6,136	$6,912	$7,665	$8,284	$9,157	$10,327	$12,116	$13,610
Subtotal Spent on Operations		$0	$2,375	$7,452	$10,127	$12,836	$13,612	$14,365	$14,984	$16,157	$17,327	$19,116	$20,610
Additional Cash Spent													
Sales Tax, VAT, HST/GST Paid Out		$0	$0	$0	$0	$0	$0	$0	$0	$0	$0	$0	$0
Principal Repayment of Current Borrowing		$0	$0	$0	$0	$0	$0	$0	$0	$0	$0	$0	$0
Other Liabilities Principal Repayment		$0	$0	$0	$0	$0	$0	$0	$0	$0	$0	$0	$0
Long-term Liabilities Principal Repayment		$700	$700	$700	$700	$700	$700	$700	$700	$700	$700	$700	$700
Purchase Other Current Assets		$0	$0	$0	$0	$0	$0	$0	$0	$0	$0	$0	$0
Purchase Long-term Assets		$0	$0	$0	$0	$0	$0	$0	$0	$0	$0	$0	$0
Dividends		$0	$0	$0	$0	$0	$0	$0	$0	$0	$0	$0	$0
Subtotal Cash Spent		$700	$3,075	$8,152	$10,827	$13,536	$14,312	$15,065	$15,684	$16,857	$18,027	$19,816	$21,310
Net Cash Flow		($700)	($3,075)	($6,152)	($5,238)	($6,709)	($5,928)	($5,468)	($4,230)	($3,112)	($573)	$413	$302
Cash Balance		$55,700	$52,625	$47,473	$42,235	$35,527	$29,599	$24,131	$19,901	$16,789	$16,216	$16,629	$16,932

Page 5

Appendix

Table: Balance Sheet

Pro Forma Balance Sheet													
Assets	Starting Balances	Month 1	Month 2	Month 3	Month 4	Month 5	Month 6	Month 7	Month 8	Month 9	Month 10	Month 11	Month 12
Current Assets													
Cash	$56,400	$55,700	$52,625	$47,473	$42,236	$35,527	$29,599	$24,131	$19,901	$16,789	$16,216	$16,629	$16,932
Inventory	$0	$0	$0	$375	$699	$853	$1,048	$1,158	$1,432	$1,718	$2,182	$2,529	$2,702
Other Current Assets	$1,500	$1,500	$1,500	$1,500	$1,500	$1,500	$1,500	$1,500	$1,500	$1,500	$1,500	$1,500	$1,500
Total Current Assets	$57,900	$57,200	$54,125	$49,348	$44,434	$37,880	$32,147	$26,830	$22,833	$20,007	$19,898	$20,658	$21,133
Long-term Assets													
Long-term Assets	$5,000	$5,000	$5,000	$5,000	$5,000	$5,000	$5,000	$5,000	$5,000	$5,000	$5,000	$5,000	$5,000
Accumulated Depreciation	$0	$83	$166	$249	$332	$415	$498	$581	$664	$747	$830	$913	$996
Total Long-term Assets	$5,000	$4,917	$4,834	$4,751	$4,668	$4,585	$4,502	$4,419	$4,336	$4,253	$4,170	$4,087	$4,004
Total Assets	$62,900	$62,117	$58,959	$54,099	$49,102	$42,465	$36,649	$31,249	$27,169	$24,260	$24,068	$24,745	$25,137
Liabilities and Capital		Month 1	Month 2	Month 3	Month 4	Month 5	Month 6	Month 7	Month 8	Month 9	Month 10	Month 11	Month 12
Current Liabilities													
Accounts Payable	$0	$536	$2,291	$5,908	$8,088	$9,038	$10,024	$10,819	$11,995	$13,536	$15,933	$17,806	$18,697
Current Borrowing	$0	$0	$0	$0	$0	$0	$0	$0	$0	$0	$0	$0	$0
Other Current Liabilities	$0	$0	$0	$0	$0	$0	$0	$0	$0	$0	$0	$0	$0
Subtotal Current Liabilities	$0	$536	$2,291	$5,908	$8,088	$9,038	$10,024	$10,819	$11,995	$13,536	$15,933	$17,806	$18,697
Long-term Liabilities	$65,000	$64,300	$63,600	$62,900	$62,200	$61,500	$60,800	$60,100	$59,400	$58,700	$58,000	$57,300	$56,600
Total Liabilities	$65,000	$64,836	$65,891	$68,808	$70,288	$70,538	$70,824	$70,919	$71,395	$72,236	$73,933	$75,106	$75,297
Paid-in Capital	$15,000	$15,000	$15,000	$15,000	$15,000	$15,000	$15,000	$15,000	$15,000	$15,000	$15,000	$15,000	$15,000
Retained Earnings	($17,100)	($17,100)	($17,100)	($17,100)	($17,100)	($17,100)	($17,100)	($17,100)	($17,100)	($17,100)	($17,100)	($17,100)	($17,100)
Earnings	$0	($619)	($4,832)	($12,609)	($19,086)	($25,973)	($32,075)	($37,571)	($42,127)	($45,876)	($47,766)	($48,261)	($48,060)
Total Capital	($2,100)	($2,719)	($6,932)	($14,709)	($21,186)	($28,073)	($34,175)	($39,671)	($44,227)	($47,976)	($49,866)	($50,361)	($50,160)
Total Liabilities and Capital	$62,900	$62,117	$58,959	$54,099	$49,102	$42,465	$36,649	$31,249	$27,169	$24,260	$24,068	$24,745	$25,137
Net Worth	($2,100)	($2,719)	($6,932)	($14,709)	($21,186)	($28,073)	($34,175)	($39,671)	($44,227)	($47,976)	($49,866)	($50,361)	($50,160)

Blue Print to build your own screen press.

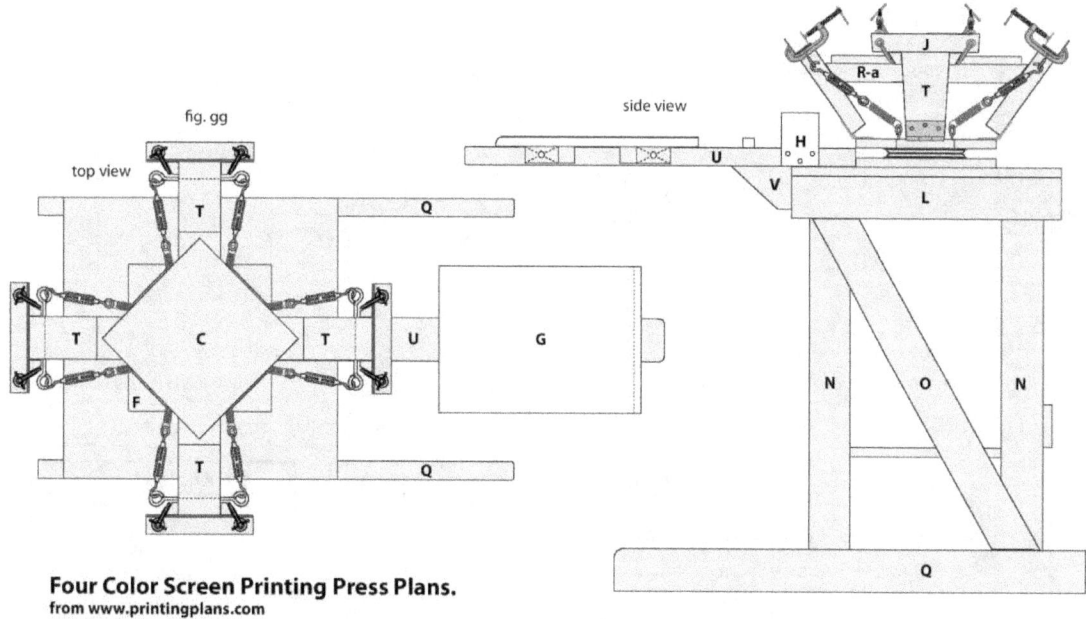

fig. gg

top view

side view

Four Color Screen Printing Press Plans.

from www.printingplans.com
Difficulty: Intermediate
Creators: Michael Phipps and Dan Mitchell
Plans Prepared by: Michael Phipps on July 8th, 2008; updated October 26th, 2009
See shirts printed on this press at http://www.ScatterbrainTees.com

All images copyright Michael Phipps. Images may be printed for private use.

This four color, one station printing press was designed and built by Michael Phipps and Dan Mitchell. It is sturdy and very precise and can be built for less than $150, which is quite a bit less than even the cheapest commercial presses. ***Save time, gas and money and buy the hardware in one package. Go to http://www.printingplans.com/hardware.html**

Plan on a few days to finish the press as it is very involved. It is recommended to have a second person help out as several steps could use one person holding while the other person attaches.

A few notes before the main instructions: The sturdiness and precision of the press is important for the success of multi-color images, so it's important to be as accurate as possible in your measurements. It is also recommended that you use wood glue at each joint in addition to screws so that the press is as stable as possible, although this makes it very difficult to UNDO steps once it's dried. You may also want to predrill holes before putting in the screws to avoid splitting of the wood (use a bit that's slightly smaller than the screw). This table is designed for a six foot tall person. To alter it for someone of a different height, adjust parts N and O accordingly.accordingly.

Tools You'll Need:
Power Drill/Screwdriver
Wood and Metal Bits
Miter Saw
Table Saw or Circular Saw
Electric Sander
Workbench Vise or Drill Press
Yardstick/Measuring Tape
Pencil
Level
Square
Clamps
Wood Glue
Welding Glue (or tools/materials for welding)
Paper or Card stock

Materials Needed:
In the diagram below you'll find the dimensions of all the lumber you'll need. The particle board can be another type of wood as long as it is ½" thick. The most important thing regarding the thickness of your wood is that the sum of the width of pieces B, F and the lazy susan turntable is ever-sol-slightly greater than the sum of the thickness of pieces I and U. This will help align everything so your screens float just the perfect height above your shirts for off-contact printing. You should be able to cut all your 2 x 4 pieces out of six 8-foot lengths, so I'd recommend buying seven to be safe. They should all be good, straight pieces, but it is especially important to find a perfectly straight piece for parts **T** and **U**.

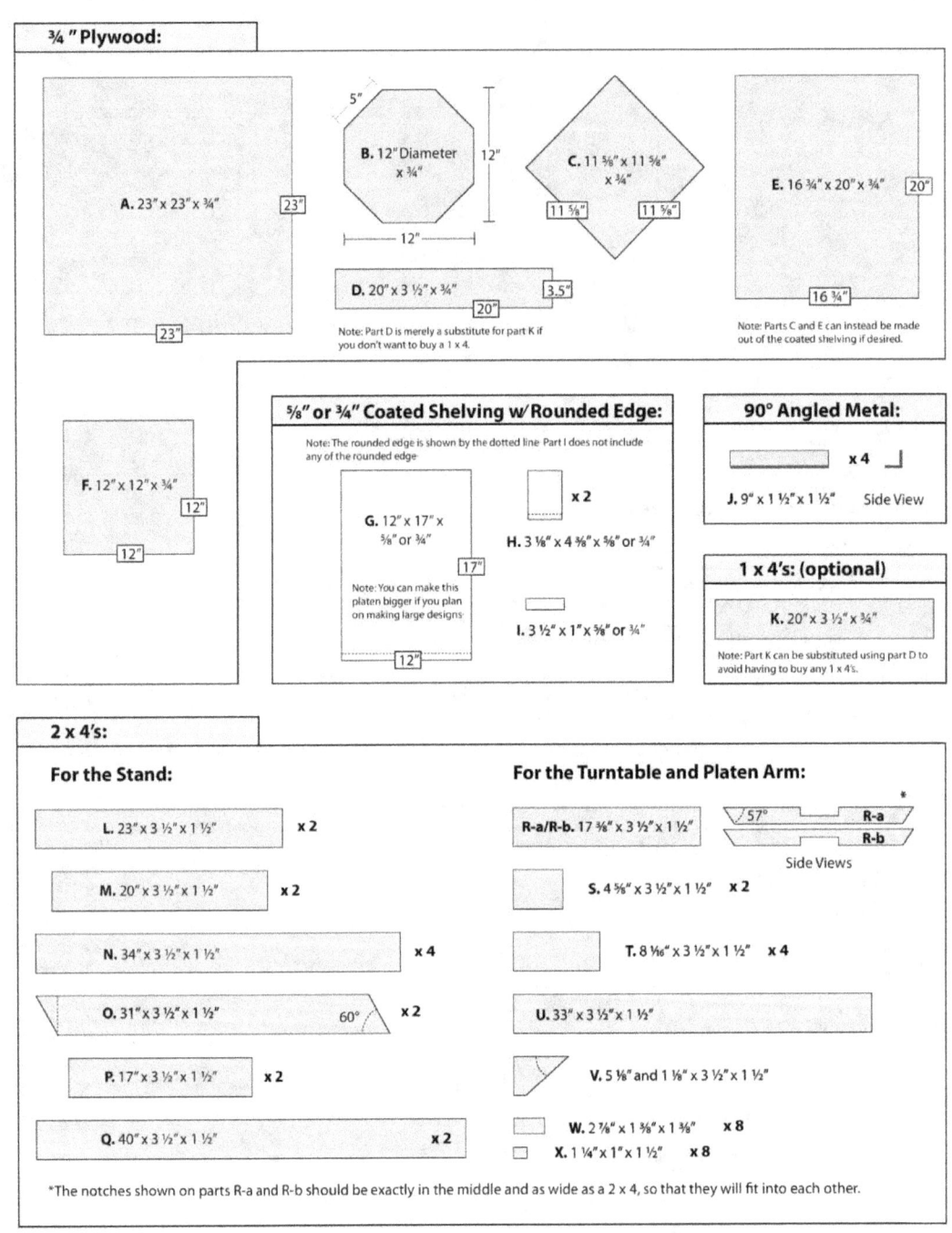

¾ " Plywood:

A. 23" x 23" x ¾" — 23" x 23"

B. 12" Diameter x ¾" — 5", 12", 12"

C. 11 ⅝" x 11 ⅝" x ¾" — 11 ⅝", 11 ⅝"

D. 20" x 3 ½" x ¾" — 20", 3.5"

Note: Part D is merely a substitute for part K if you don't want to buy a 1 x 4.

E. 16 ¾" x 20" x ¾" — 20", 16 ¾"

Note: Parts C and E can instead be made out of the coated shelving if desired.

F. 12" x 12" x ¾" — 12", 12"

⅝" or ¾" Coated Shelving w/ Rounded Edge:

Note: The rounded edge is shown by the dotted line. Part I does not include any of the rounded edge.

G. 12" x 17" x ⅝" or ¾" — 17", 12"

Note: You can make this platen bigger if you plan on making large designs.

H. 3 ⅛" x 4 ⅜" x ⅝" or ¾" — x 2

I. 3 ½" x 1" x ⅝" or ¾"

90° Angled Metal:

J. 9" x 1 ½" x 1 ½"   Side View   x 4

1 x 4's: (optional)

K. 20" x 3 ½" x ¾"

Note: Part K can be substituted using part D to avoid having to buy any 1 x 4's.

2 x 4's:

For the Stand:

L. 23" x 3 ½" x 1 ½"   x 2

M. 20" x 3 ½" x 1 ½"   x 2

N. 34" x 3 ½" x 1 ½"   x 4

O. 31" x 3 ½" x 1 ½"   60°   x 2

P. 17" x 3 ½" x 1 ½"   x 2

Q. 40" x 3 ½" x 1 ½"   x 2

For the Turntable and Platen Arm:

R-a/R-b. 17 ⅜" x 3 ½" x 1 ½"   57°   R-a   R-b   Side Views

S. 4 ⅜" x 3 ½" x 1 ½"   x 2

T. 8 ⅛" x 3 ½" x 1 ½"   x 4

U. 33" x 3 ½" x 1 ½"

V. 5 ⅛" and 1 ⅛" x 3 ½" x 1 ½"

W. 2 ⅞" x 1 ⅜" x 1 ⅜"   x 8

X. 1 ¼" x 1" x 1 ½"   x 8

*The notches shown on parts R-a and R-b should be exactly in the middle and as wide as a 2 x 4, so that they will fit into each other.

Hardware Needed:

approx. 1 # 2" Wood Screws (You can use 2.5" for most of these, but you'll need some 2" for the platen and other areas)
6   2.5" to 3" Wood Screws (Use these for diagonal screws in parts V and O)
8   Metal C-Clamps, 2" x 1" (The first dimension is the max. clamping width, the second is the depth)
4   Hinges with hardware (screws), 3 ½" wide
8   Hook & Eye Turnbuckles, ³⁄₁₆" x 4"
8   Springs, ⅜" x 3 ¼" x .072" (Resorte/Ressort brand has these exact measurements)
8   Lag Eye Screws, ¼" x 3 ¾"
4   Lag Eye Screws, ³⁄₁₆" x 1 ⅜" or 2 ¹⁄₁₆"
4   Hex Cap Bolts, ¼" x 1 ¼"
4   Hex Cap Bolts, ¼" x 1 ¾"
2   Hex Cap Bolts, ⅜" x 6 ¾" or 7""
2   Carriage Bolts, ⅜" x 3"
8   Hex Nuts, ¼"
2   Hex Nuts, ⅜"
4   Washers, ¼"
6   Washers, ⅜"
8   Fender Washers (These need to be 1 ¼" diameter)
2   Wingnuts, ⅜"
1   Lazy Susan Turntable, 6" x 6" x ¾" (This is the only item in this list you are not likely to find in a regular hardware store. You will need to go to a woodworking supply store as they stock these for rotating barstools. Don't skimp on this- it needs to be sturdy and have no slop.)

Making the table:

Step 1: Cut all your lumber, marking each piece with the appropriate letter to make assembly easier. We'll start by assembling the table itself. First, lay down parts **L** and **Q** and attach the legs (part N) as shown (fig. a). Make sure that your angles are perfectly square. Where parts L extend past the legs, use a piece of 2 x 4 to check that the bits that extend are exactly equal to the smaller width of the wood.

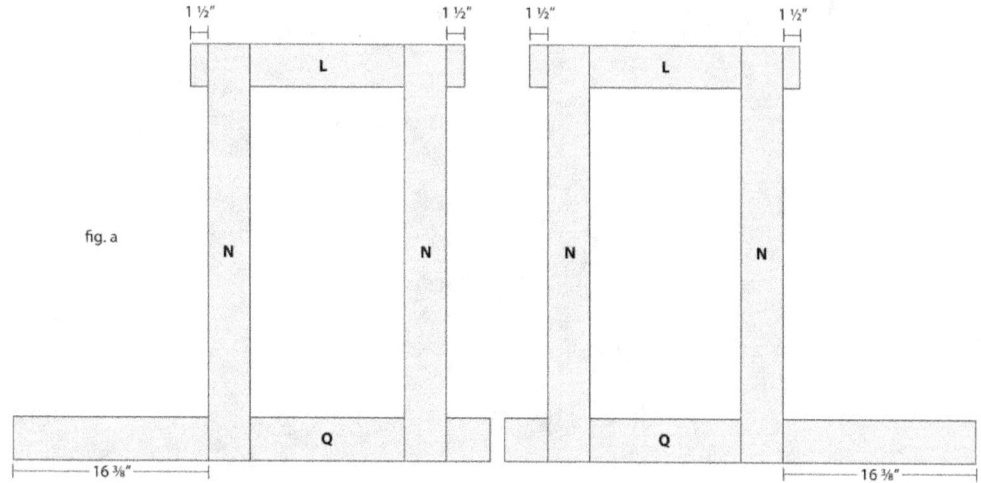

fig. a

Step 2: Attach the thin sides of parts **M** to part **A** as shown in **fig. b**. Use only glue and clamps for now. Again using only clamps and glue, set parts **A** and **M** on top of the two legs you built in Step 1, so that parts **L** and **M** form a square around the perimeter of **A**. This is shown from above in **fig. c**. (Dotted lines indicate parts beneath.) Once you feel comfortable with the fit, Go ahead and screw parts **L** into **M**, and **A** into both **L** & **M** from the top.

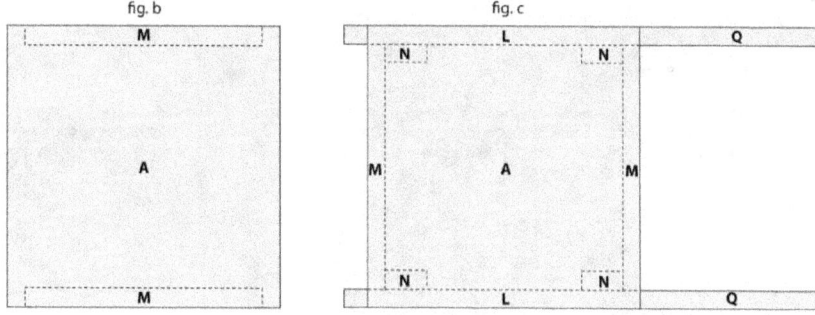

fig. b   fig. c

Step 3: Now you have a standing, albeit weak, table. Attach parts **P** to legs **N** as shown in **fig. d**. Do it in the front and back, both times keeping part **P** flush to the outside, as seen from above in **fig. e**. Note: Parts **P** act as a support beam and rests for a shelf (part **E**). It can be lowered or raised to suit your preference, and additional shelves may be added if desired.

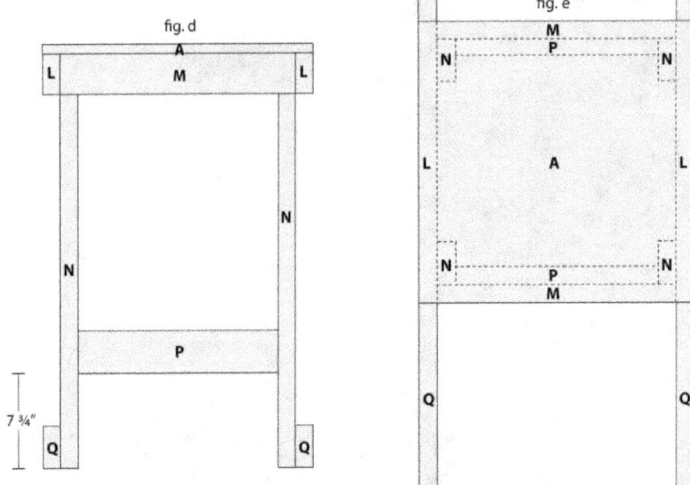

fig. d

fig. e

Step 4: Attach part **O** to the outside of both sides of the table (**fig. f**). Make sure you orient them as shown for maximum support. Now secure shelf **E** onto crossbeams **P** to act as a shelf. Add part **K** to the back to help keep items from falling off. You are now finished with the table itself. It should be plenty sturdy with no give at all.

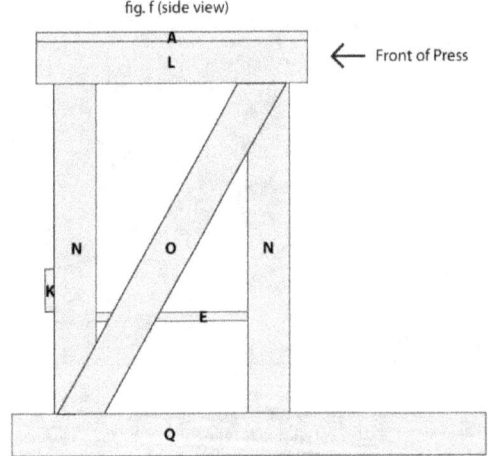

fig. f (side view)

← Front of Press

Building the Platen Arm and Platen:

Step 5: The platen arm is the board that extends from the table and on which a board (the platen) is placed, over which shirts are pulled and printed. First glue piece **F** in the exact middle of the top of the table (piece **A**). This can be done by drawing lines from opposite corners on piece **A**, (creating an "X"). Now by matching the corners of board **F** onto the newly drawn "X", you'll get it in the middle (see fig. g). Do not screw it in place at this time- use glue only.

fig. g

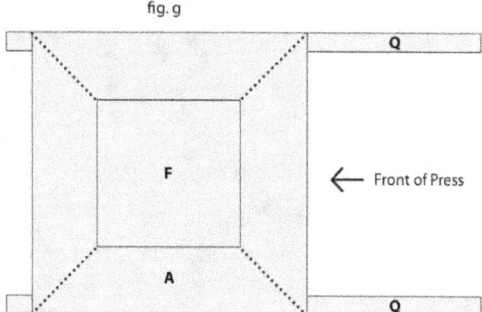

← Front of Press

Step 6: Before continuing with the press itself, we're going to build the platen. The platen featured here is for adult T-shirts, so if you're interested in printing other types of items you'll need to build other platens of different sizes. This design is such that you can use the platen sideways for wide designs in addition to using it in its normal position. If that it not of interest to you, just don't cut and attach parts W-b. (After a year and a half of having this press, I personally haven't used it sideways, but have built larger, additional platens for wide designs.)

Using your drill press or workbench vise and drill, create half-inch holes in the middle of the largest side of 4 of your parts **W**. For the remaining 4, draw a line 2 ⅜" in from the end and drill the holes in the new middle (see **fig. h**). Then attach them onto board **G** as shown in fig. i. Use a 2 x 4 to help you space the wood so the platen will fit snugly onto the platen arm when it's ready. Also make sure that the distance between the holes in one direction is the exact same distance as the holes going the other way (see **fig. j**). You'll definitely want to predrill your holes before attaching parts **W** or you'll have problems with splitting wood.

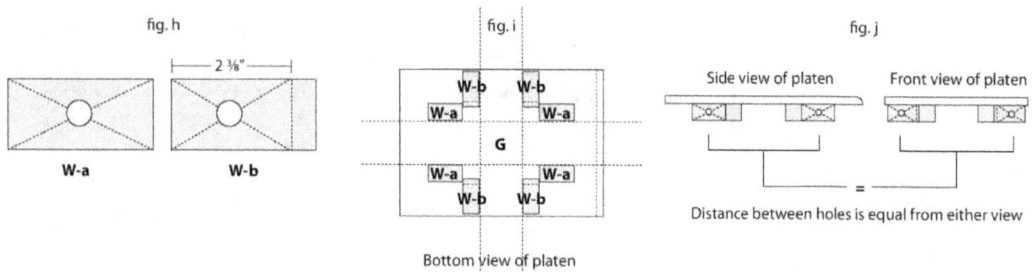

Step 7: Now that you have a finished platen, let's use it to determine where to drill holes in your platen arm (part **U**). Place the platen over the part **U** (it should fit snuggly). The curved edge of the platen should be 3" from the end of the platen arm. Mark the holes, remove the platen, then drill half-inch holes throught the platen arm, making sure that they go straight through. You may also want to drill a second set of holes 2 ¼" further in (to the left if looking at **fig. k**) for greater flexibility when printing.

fig. k

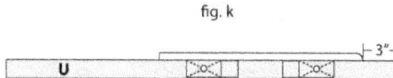

Step 8: Now that the holes are drilled in the platen arm, let's attach it to the table. Use your two carriage bolts with the appropriate washers and hex nuts to attach it and add four screws for added stability. See **fig l** for placement. The dotted lines indicate where to measure to insure your platen arm is straight (before securing). Attach part **V** as shown in **fig. m** so it's centered in the middle of part **U**. Make sure the screws go into the table AND the platen arm.

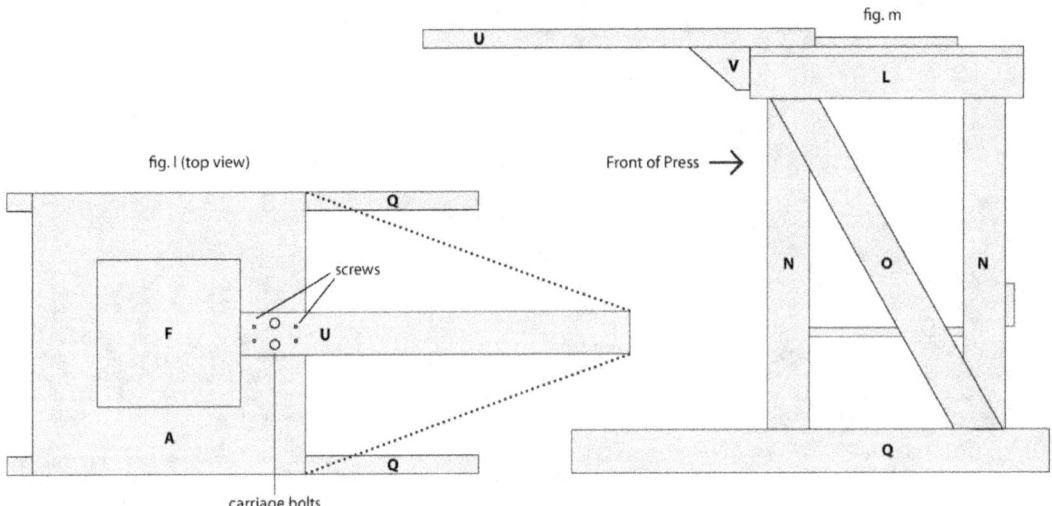

fig. m

fig. l (top view)

Front of Press →

screws

carriage bolts

Building the Rotating Printing Press:

Step 9: Attach your "Lazy Susan Turntable" directly in the middle of part **F** using 4 of your 1 ¾" hex cap bolts. Drill holes directly through parts **F** and **A** to do this and use hex nuts to secure them underneath. **Fig. n** shows this as if the top part of the turntable is missing, just so you can see the orientation of the hex cap bolts. Draw an X onto part B by dividing it in half and in half again. Make sure this is exactly in the center. You'll be using this later. Next glue both parts **S** back to back and attach the end of the resulting block to the middle of part **B**. See **fig. o** for two views of this.

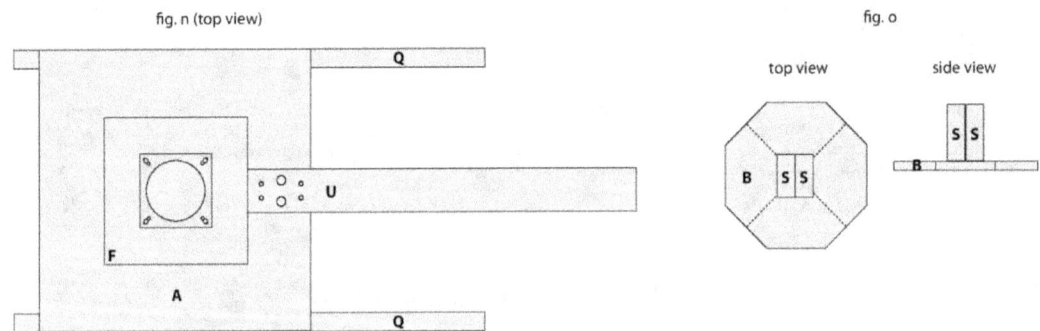

fig. n (top view)

fig. o

top view   side view

Step 10: Your accuracy in the following steps is vital to the success of your finished product, so measure carefully! Drill holes in each of your metal brackets as shown in **fig. p**. Now use a larger bit equal to the size of your screw heads and drill in each of your holes, so that when you screw the bracket on, the screw heads will be flush. Attach each bracket to the end of a part **T**, making sure it's in the exact middle from side to side. The vertical position of the bracket depends on the width of your coated lumber (used for the platen). If you are using 3/4" thick wood for your platen, the bracket should extend past the bottom of part **T** the thickness of your hinge. (**fig. q**). If you are using 5/8" thick wood for your platen, place the brackets an ADDITIONAL 1/8" down past part T. On the opposite end of each part **T**, screw in one of the hinges so that the edge of the cylindrical part of the hinge is flush with the edge of board **T**. Use the screws that came with the hinge. The hinge should be facing "up", so that when you put in the screws from the bottom into the wood, it will be through the "wrong" end. In other words, the tapered part of the hole is now between the hinge and the wood, and the larger part of the cylindrical section of the hinge is facing up (**figs. q & r**).

fig. p

fig. q

side view

Step 11: Now attach each arm (part **T** with additions) to four sides of part **B** using the rest of the screws that came with the hinges (fig. s). Make sure that "length y" is the same for all arms. Using the "X" you drew onto part **B** in step 9, measure in 2 ¼" from each side and drill a hole big enough for your ³⁄₁₆" hex cap bolts.

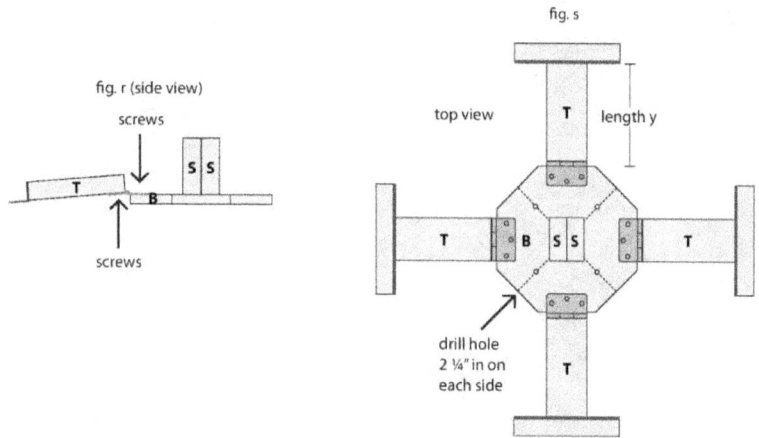

fig. s

fig. r (side view)

screws

top view

T

length y

screws

drill hole 2 ¼" in on each side

Step 12: Bolt the piece you just built in step 11 to the lazy suzan turntable using ¼" hex cap bolts from underneath and the appropriate nuts and washers. Make sure all four arms reach the exact same spot on the platen arm (as shown in **fig. t**). You can probably move the whole top part slightly until this is the case, and then tighten the nuts. If you can't seem to get each arm to the same spot on part **U**, tighten the nuts when you've done the best you can. You still need to get the arms the same length, so mark the shortest one, remove part **J** from any arm that is longer, and sand part **T** until it's the appropriate length. Now reattach any part **J** that was removed. This may seem like a lot of extra work, but it will be well worth it once you start printing multi-color shirts.

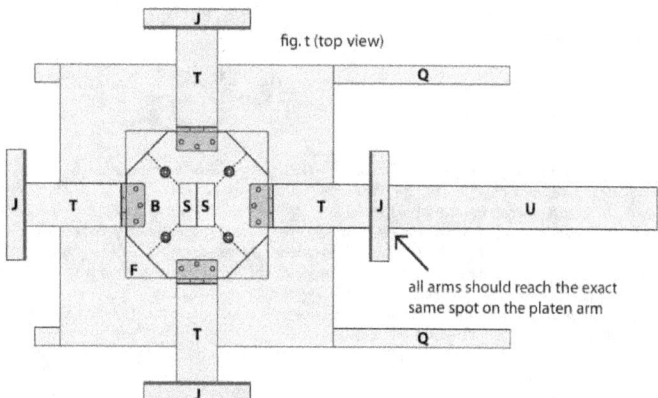

fig. t (top view)

all arms should reach the exact same spot on the platen arm

Step 13: Twist the top mechanism 45° to get it out of the way (this will become easier when we add the springs so the arms will be out of the way). If it won't twist because it binds on part **U**, sand enough of the inner end of part **U** off until there is no obstruction. Attach part **I** onto the platen arm (**U**) using a single screw (otherwise it would probably split). It should be right where part **J** lands when you lay an arm onto part **U**, or about 8 ⅝" in from the inner end of part **U** (see **figs. u** and **v**). Next attach parts **H** to the platen arm (part **U**) so that the curved part of the board is on top and faces in, and so that parts **H** overhang ⅞" over the side of part **A**. Make sure to predrill holes for the screws (slightly small than the screws) to make this easier. See figs. **u**, **v** and **w** for different views of this.

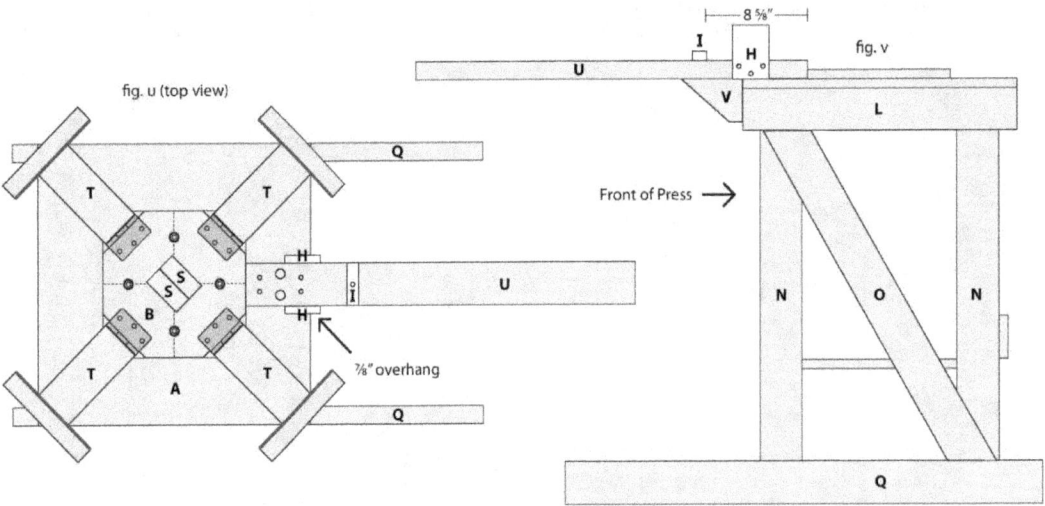

fig. u (top view)

fig. v

8 ⅝"

Front of Press →

⅞" overhang

Step 13 (continued): **Fig. w** shows boards **H** with the curved parts facing in. The reason for this is that as you lower an arm into place, the curved edges will help it fall easily into place. Try doing this now to make sure there is the correct width between the two parts **H**. The arm (**T**) should fit VERY snuggly, but stil be able to go into place without excessive force. Remember that when you have a screen connected to the arm it will become even easier to do this because of leverage. Getting parts **H** to be the perfect distance apart was one of the most difficult parts of building my own press. At first it was too tight and required some adjustment. To make these fine adjustments, loosen the screws and use pieces of cardstock as shims in between parts **H** and **U**. Then retighten the screws. Add more shims as necessary until you have the perfect width. If you take the time to do this, you're press will be ultra-accurate.

fig. w (top view)

H H
U

Step 14: Now that you've secured the brackets (**H**), you can use them to hold each arm (**T**) in place while you do the next step. On each arm, draw a line 1 ³⁄₁₆" in from the outer edge of part **T** (see **fig. x**). Using these as guides, screw in each of your ¼" lag eye screws into parts **T** until they only stick out about 2 ¼" from the board. Next screw in your set of four smaller lag eye screws into part **B**, halfway between the bolts that are already on the dotted line and parts **S**. See **fig. x** for the proper orientation of the lag eye screws. Now gather all your springs and turnbuckles. You're now going to connect one spring to the closed end of each turnbuckle. If the ends of the springs are closed instead of hooks, clamp one pair of vise grips onto the end of a spring as indicated by the red bar in **fig. y**. Next use your other pair of vise grips and grasp the same end of the spring as indicated by the blue bar. Now as you bring the two pairs of vise grips together it will widen the opening. Once the opening is wide enough, remove the vise grips and attach the spring to the eye end of the turnbuckle. Now use a single pair of vise grips to sqeeze the openings on the end of the springs closed. Do this to all 8 sets of springs and turnbuckles (see **fig. y**).

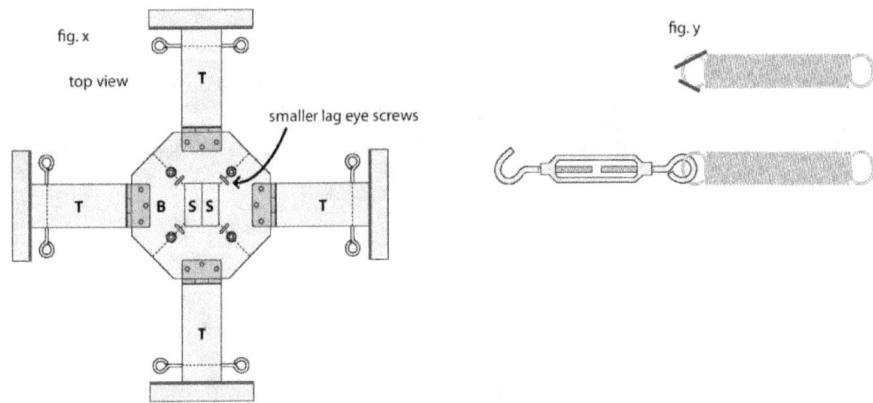

fig. x

top view

smaller lag eye screws

fig. y

Step 15: Now attach each of your turnbuckle/spring combos to the top rotating mechanism. The hooks will attach to the large lag eye screws at ends of the arms, and the loose ends of the springs will attach to the lag eye screws sticking out of the octoganal part **B** (two springs per lag screw). You'll need to use the vise grips to attach the springs as before. We'll adjust the tension of the turnbuckles later on. You can push each arm down so it touches the table to keep it out of the way while you work. Now take each of your C-clamps and drill a hole in the the main arm 1" up from the the point shown in **fig. aa**. [Clamp shown is a 2.5" clamp. You can use 2" clamps just as effectively.] This hole should be just slightly smaller than one of your screw heads. After you've done this to all eight, weld your 1" or 1 ¼" diameter washers to the mobile part of the clamp as shown. Welding glue will work just fine. Put cardboard in between the washer and the adjacent part of the clamp to avoid bonding the clamp to itself. The purpose of these washers is to create a greater surface area on the clamp so as to avoid denting your screen frames.

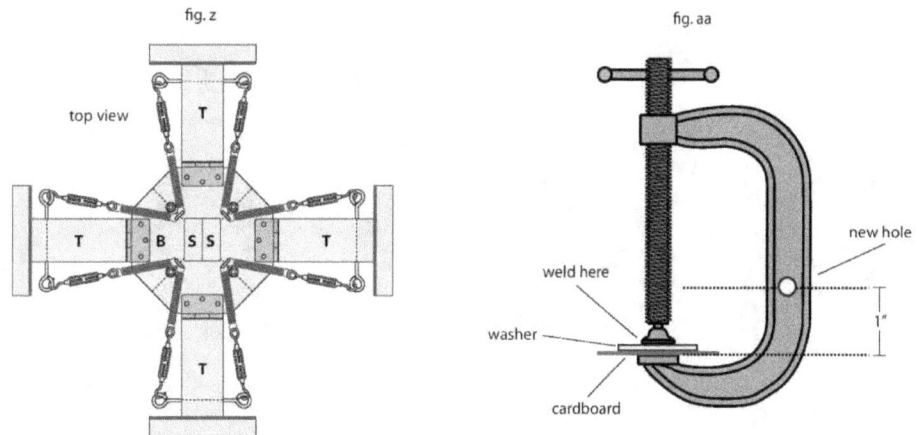

fig. z

fig. aa

Step 16: **(Note: Fig bb** shows what to do with 2" clamps, **fig. cc** with 2.5" clamps.) Once the welding glue dries, and using **figs. bb** (or **cc**) **and dd** as your guides, screw your altered C-clamps through parts **X** into part **T**. (You'll want to have parts **X** glued and clamped to make this easier.) The washers that you welded onto the C-clamps need to clear the side of the vertical part of bracket **J**. The bottom of the C-clamps can be welded (glued) underneath brackets **J** as shown in **fig cc.**, but this is optional. Tighten the clamps all the way while you work and while it glues to help hold them in place. Not only will your C-clamps hold your screens firmly in place, but they will also act as a place to rest your squeegees when your screens are in an upright position.

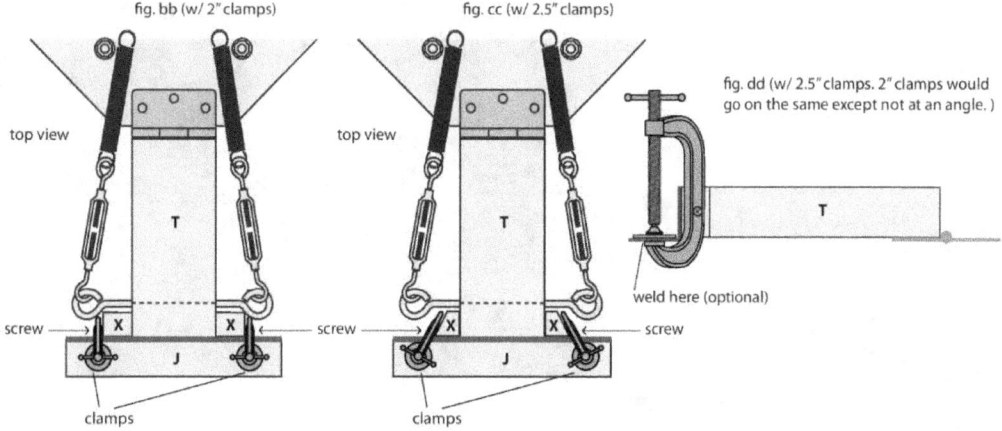

fig. bb (w/ 2" clamps)

fig. cc (w/ 2.5" clamps)

fig. dd (w/ 2.5" clamps. 2" clamps would go on the same except not at an angle.)

Step 17: Part **R-a** has a notch on the top, part **R-b** has a notch on the bottom. Glue part **R-b** onto part **R-a** so the notches intersect, forming an "X". Attach this "X" onto the top of parts **S** so that it is centered, as shown in figs. **ee** and **ff**.

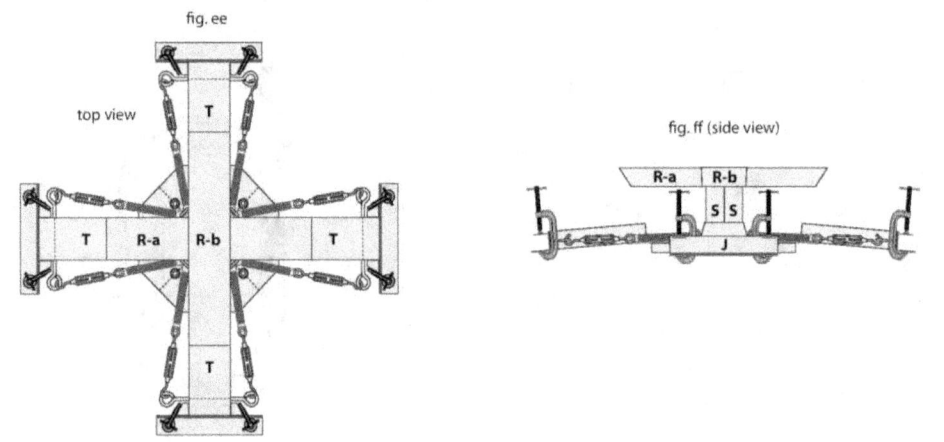

fig. ee

top view

fig. ff (side view)

Step 18: Next attach shelf **C** onto the top so that the corners are each in the middle of parts **R** (see **fig. gg**). Now sand off the corners protruding from parts **Q** and **U**. Not only will this save you some potential pain as you print, but the smooth end of the platen arm will help shirts slide on more easily.

20" x 24" frames work best with this press. Attach a frame to each arm (one at a time) and place a squeegee on it. Now that you've got it at its operation weight, it's time to adjust the turnbuckles so it will gently return back to the upright position in between pulls (if released about half way up). For each arm, make sure you adjust the two turnbuckles equally until you are happy with the tension. If your press squeaks when the arms are lowered, use a little WD40 on the insides of parts H. That's it. You're done! Happy printing!

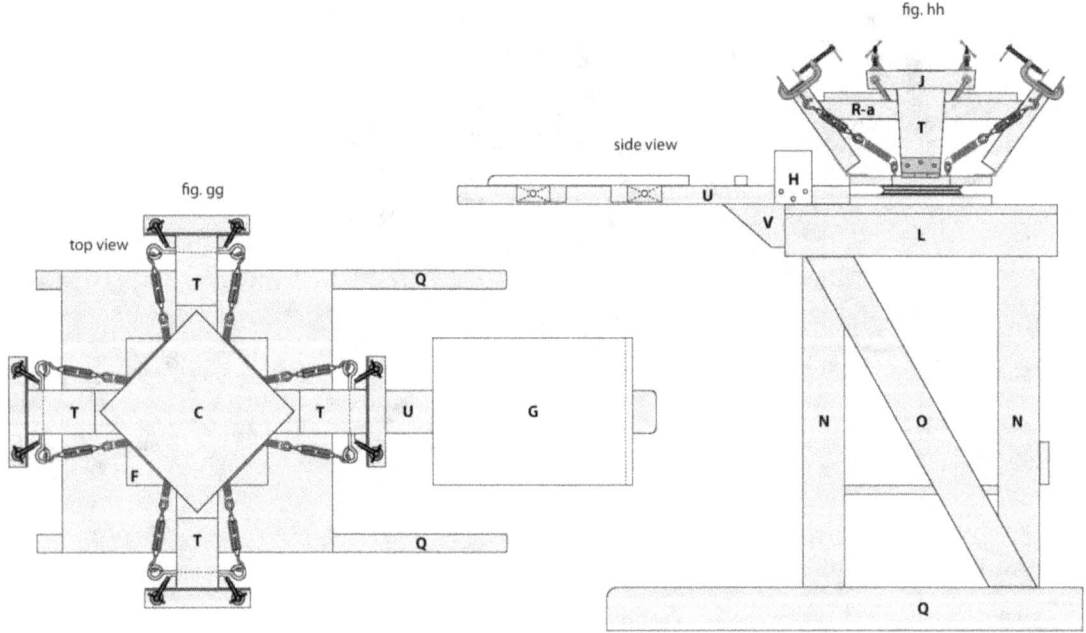

fig. hh

side view

fig. gg

top view

ACKNOWLEDGEMENTS

This book is for the dreamer who wants to work for themselves. I would like to thank the reader also I our editor Donna Jackson.